東京三越吳服店

The World of Department Stores

Jan Whitaker

THE VENDOME PRESS

NEW YORK

Contents

Wonders of the World

Rarely are businesses showered with the kind of superlatives usually reserved for spectacular canyons or medieval cathedrals. Yet in 1870s' and 1880s' Paris, department stores were touted as the "eighth wonder of the world."[1] They held a powerful attraction for tourists and locals alike, and their allure persists to this day. The love affair with the department store has proven a hardy one. Even as the Depression of the 1930s eroded its profits and pushed it to the brink of failure, the Marshall Field store in Chicago was not simply a shopping mecca but, as *Fortune* magazine declared, "an elementary fact of existence."[2] Today, many department stores have encountered threats to their prosperity, but people still treasure them as representing a more gracious style of commerce.

Anyone who delves into the history of department stores cannot help but conclude that they have been a monumental factor in modern life and that their influence goes far beyond the sale of merchandise. Writing in 1995, historian William Lancaster observed, "Department stores have existed for so long that they have become embedded into our psyche and they form an integral part of the pattern of everyday life."[3] In wartime, department stores represent a haven of normalcy, as expressed, perhaps most famously, by the Chicago woman who commented, after the bombing of Pearl Harbor, "Nothing is left any more—except, thank God, Marshall Field's."[4] Residents of Tokyo had a similar reaction at the end of World War II. Amid the rubble of the Ginza in 1945, department stores, damaged and with little merchandise to sell, were reduced to doing business on one floor. Yet shoppers poured in to buy Japanese prints, not because they wanted or needed them but because it was the first time in two years that the stores had been open for business.[5] Their centrality to people's lives explains in part why so many department stores continue on, their centenary anniversaries ten, twenty, even fifty years behind them.

Though no longer the economic giants they were in the late nineteenth and early twentieth centuries, when they dominated retailing, department stores remained significant businesses for decades. In 1913 two Paris department stores were listed among the top forty publicly held companies in France, the only businesses outside of finance, transportation, utilities, and heavy industry to attain that level.[6] The big stores, often a city's largest employer, gave work to thousands. Picture, for instance, the mighty spectacle of 6,500 employees of Philadelphia's John Wanamaker store marching before a reviewing stand in the store's grand court in 1911 to the strains of the hymn "Onward Christian Soldiers."[7]

Their economic roles were diverse. Department stores stabilized and bolstered real estate values in the centers of Tokyo, Toronto, London, and other major cities. In Berlin the big Tietz and Wertheim stores maintained the value of the old shopping street when commercial activity shifted to Leipziger and Potsdamer streets. Department-store advertising helped build a revenue base for newspapers in the nineteenth century and formed the advertising backbone of the industry for much of the twentieth.

As for merchandise, there is scarcely a category of consumer goods that they have not carried at some time or other, from ribbons and feathers to automobiles and airplanes. Charles Dickens, eldest son of the author, described how London's Whiteley, the "universal provider," was prepared to cater to all his material wants from infancy to old age, until finally "the Provider secures me an eligible spot for my resting-place."[8] Harrods provided a similar funerary service, and Japan's Mitsukoshi department store introduced one in 1977.[9]

Department-store innovations led the retailing revolution. By purchasing large orders directly from manufacturers, and sometimes engaging in manufacturing themselves, they were able to

lower prices, making products affordable to consumers previously excluded from the marketplace. Even their enemies, small merchants and producers who felt threatened, had to acknowledge that they were impressive institutions. "They get the crowd; they cut prices; they are modern; they are open to every innovation," ruefully admitted a spokesperson for independent booksellers, who were being crushed by department-store price-cutting.[10]

Under the guidance of department stores, the modern consumer began to evolve. The stores convinced consumers that it made more sense to buy manufactured goods than to make them at home. Department-store merchandise raised consumers' standards and broadened their material wants. People who had never set foot in a bookstore bought books; sales of black tea soared after the stores served free samples in tea nooks; conservative women began to wear costume jewelry. The stores took careful note of consumer preferences and advised manufacturers on how to make products more useful and appealing.

Shopping, once an arduous and nerve-racking task, began to be enjoyed as a leisure pursuit. Luxurious and convenient, the big stores provided meals, child care, repair services, concerts, lending libraries, and restrooms furnished with comfortable chairs, desks, and free stationery. For women, the department store served as a social headquarters, a place to meet friends and relax between appointments. It became "to the housewife what his clubhouse is to the business man," said architect Louis Parnes.[11]

Children were not only beneficiaries of department stores but also targets of marketing research. No effort was spared to define the needs and desires of this large, undeveloped consumer base. By creating fairyland toy departments, playgrounds, zoos, holiday festivities, and children's meals and menus, the department store became "a shrine to the child" and helped to "construct a new culture of childhood."[12]

Department stores gathered together under one roof not only all sorts of merchandise but all sorts of people. The mixing of classes they encouraged was unprecedented in the class-segregated societies of the nineteenth century. Although there were limits on how far the stores' welcome extended, they greatly exceeded other gathering spots in providing egalitarian spaces "where the duchess and the fish-wife rub elbows."[13] For anyone aspiring to climb the status ladder, the department store was an educator that translated and transferred upper-class ways of life to other classes. Especially in America, with its large immigrant population, department stores helped raise the standard of living. In Japan, the stores educated shoppers not only about social class but also about Western goods and Western ways, if always with a Japanese flavor.

The department store has often been likened to a museum. It introduced people to the fine arts as well as to a range of unfamiliar ideas and styles. Its cultural impact was especially strong in the nineteenth century, when museums had little idea of how to present art and artifacts to the public. Undoubtedly, until recent decades people have viewed more art exhibits, listened to more concerts, and absorbed more lessons in design and taste in department stores than in public exhibition and concert halls. And for the many who experienced their first restaurant meal, escalator ride, telephone call, or fashion show in a department store, it functioned as a museum of social occasion and modern technology.

As symbols of progress, department stores have succeeded and survived for so long because they've always ridden the waves of industrial development and modern life. For decades their success depended on the growth of cities, mass transportation, and a flourishing middle class, whose ranks they helped swell and whose way of life they so profoundly influenced. May they endure.

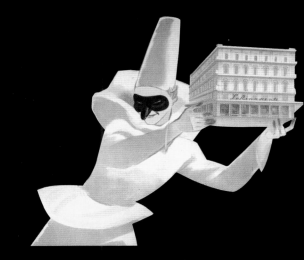

A World of Department St

Historians agree that the three key factors in the birth and development of department stores were urbanization, mass transportation, and mass production, but all three had to be present at once and working together. Not all of the world's major cities had an environment conducive to department-store growth. Beijing, for instance, the largest city in 1800, was not the kind of place where a department store would flourish—not in that century or even in the next.

In contrast, Paris, another of the world's largest cities in the nineteenth century, offered a highly nourishing environment for department stores. It had just the right mix of economic and population growth, as well as an inimitable style and verve that attracted visitors from around the globe. And with the implementation of Baron Haussmann's rational city plan of long, straight boulevards, parks, squares, and railway stations in the second half of the nineteenth century, its attraction was substantially heightened. Assisted further by an improved transportation system, visitors poured into the city. The new streets had been tailor made, it seemed, for café hoppers and window shoppers.

In the United States there were fewer barriers to the growth of department stores. There were no medieval walls to tear down, and most cities were built on a grid from the start. Although the country remained predominantly rural into the twentieth century, by the later nineteenth century there were enough large cities to furnish a healthy medium for commerce. New York, in 1860 the country's largest city, with almost 1,750,000 people, nearly tripled in size by 1900. Philadelphia more than doubled, while Chicago, the second largest city by 1890, grew fifteen fold. Boston and St. Louis more than tripled in size from 1860 to 1900, and Baltimore mushroomed by a factor of almost nine. These were the cities where America's department stores would first take hold.

As the first industrialized nation, England experienced urban growth early, and by 1900 London had become the world's largest city. Little wonder that Harry Gordon Selfridge, a retired Marshall Field's executive, chose London after scouting possible locations for a big store. He discovered that the city, nearly 6,500,000 strong in 1900, had ten million people within easy commuting distance of his chosen site.

After London and Paris, Berlin was Europe's third largest city at this time, and Germany's other large cities—Hamburg, Leipzig, Munich, Dresden, Breslau, Cologne, and the like—were also growing rapidly. In 1903 Prussia alone, though smaller in area than Texas, contained more than half as many cities with populations over 100,000 as the entire United States.

ABOVE LEFT AND RIGHT During the reign of Napoleon III, pictured on a medallion from the Universal Exposition of 1855 (inset), wide boulevards were created that sped traffic to Paris's principal attractions such as department stores.

In the more fortunate cities, rising urban populations were matched by higher incomes and standards of living, producing the middle class, which would make up the primary market for department stores. In Tokyo, the middle class made up only 4 percent of the population in 1915 but would triple in the next ten years.[1] Japanese incomes grew rapidly in the 1960s, causing department store sales to nearly double between 1963 and 1968, years in which they were shrinking in the United States.[2]

Department stores and world's fairs developed in tandem, the latter taking place on average every two years between 1855 and World War I.[3] The great world's fairs, at which nations showcased their bounty of manufactured goods, acted as a stimulus and inspiration for the very concept of the department store, and served as a model for its architecture and methods of display. The mix of goods showcased at fairs, combined with the millions of visitors who came to see them, was impossible for an enterprising merchant to ignore. William Whiteley, founder of London's first big store, was one of the six million who attended the exhibits at London's Crystal Palace in 1851. Struck by the extraordinary appeal of seeing quantities of massed goods, he wanted to create a similar effect in which the goods were not merely on display but for sale.[4] In other cities where fairs were planned, merchants saw potential customers in the huge numbers of fairgoers. The Hôtel du Louvre in Paris, site of the department store of the same name—Grands Magasins du Louvre—was built for visitors to Paris's fair of 1855, which drew 4.5 million people. Additions to the Bon Marché were timed to coincide with the 1867 fair, which drew more than 9 million visitors. Paris stores grew with the huge influx of visitors to later fairs as well: 16 million to the 1878 fair; 32 million in 1889; and 50 million in 1900.[5] Marshall Field began a large addition to his store when the announcement was made that Chicago would host a fair commemorating Columbus's discovery of America in the early 1890s. The news set off a building boom on State Street that included a trio of new department stores.[6]

Advances in transportation also stimulated department-store growth. Railroads made it possible to bring not only manufactured goods into cities but also customers from outlying areas. In big cities, horse-drawn trolleys of the mid-nineteenth century ferried people formerly confined to their neighborhoods to central shopping districts. By 1860 Paris's horse-drawn omnibuses transported over seventy million passengers a year. In Chicago, the bustling State Street shopping area developed as an outgrowth of the cable cars of the 1880s, which made their loop there, a word transferred to the area itself. By 1918 Tokyo's one hundred miles of

For detailed Advertisement see page 22.

Dry goods formed the base for many businesses that would grow into department stores.

OPPOSITE London's Swan & Edgar specialized in silks and custom dressmaking in the 1870s.

RIGHT La Cour Batave in Paris handled white cotton goods. The lush fabrics in this 1910 advertisement recall descriptions of silk displays in Émile Zola's *Au Bonheur des dames*.

street railways were capable of carrying two million people to the area where the Mitsukoshi store was located. So many people passed through Tokyo's railway terminals that they too were destined to become major shopping hubs with their own department stores. Trolleybuses running between cities and towns in the United States made it feasible to run a profitable department-store business even in rural areas. A store in Clinton, Iowa, "The Gateway of the Corn, Hog and Cattle Belt," a city with a population of about 26,000 in 1910, was able to draw from a customer base of 75,000 within a thirty-mile radius because of efficient trolley service.[7] Why department stores did not develop in cities in all parts of the world is a nagging question, not fully answered by any of the research that's been done so far. Whereas Paris, London, New York, Chicago, Philadelphia, and Berlin can be noted for their flourishing department-store cultures, Rome, Vienna, Athens, Istanbul, and Budapest cannot. A partial explanation is suggested by a store proposed in Iowa.

Right after the turn of the last century a group of businessmen planned a department store for Des Moines, Iowa, population 85,000. On an envelope they listed all of the city's characteristics that they thought would contribute to a department store's success. Unfortunately for them, the store was not built, undoubtedly a victim of the tight credit of the 1906 recession, but their list singles out factors favorable to large-scale commercial development. They assessed the city's economic vitality by its "immense" jobbing and wholesale trade and its forty-four insurance companies, nineteen banks, and two hundred fifty major factories. Des Moines' post office did a business equal to cities twice its size. Resources included cheap coal, a hundred miles of gas mains, ten thousand telephones in use, six express companies, two telegraph companies, and a total of fifty-four newspapers and periodicals, including three major dailies. The citizens were well educated, and there were thirteen colleges and technical schools. Eighty annual conventions plus the Iowa State Fair attracted thousands to the city each year and accommodated them in its twenty-eight hotels. And the city had good roads, ninety-six miles of electric railway tracks, and interurban trolleys running outside the city in all four directions.[8]

Important as they are, economic factors alone don't seem to explain everything. Why, for instance, did London lag behind Paris, which is widely regarded as the birthplace of the department store? Why did department stores thrive in the United States, even in cities far smaller than many in Europe that had no department stores? In Paris there was an undeniable—and indefinable—cultural aspect that made it the premier shopping city, and it clearly had something

BELOW To the right is the Grands Magasins du Louvre, while to the left is the Hotel du Louvre from which it originated. A principal activity of the women in the hotel was shopping, and they came from all over the world to acquire the styles of the great fashion capital.

OPPOSITE, TOP Berlin's premier department store of the 20th century, Wertheim, at Leipziger Platz.

OPPOSITE, BOTTOM Cover of a brochure celebrating the 60th anniversary of the Nathan Israel women's specialty store, Berlin, 1926. Many department stores in Germany were owned by Jewish families.

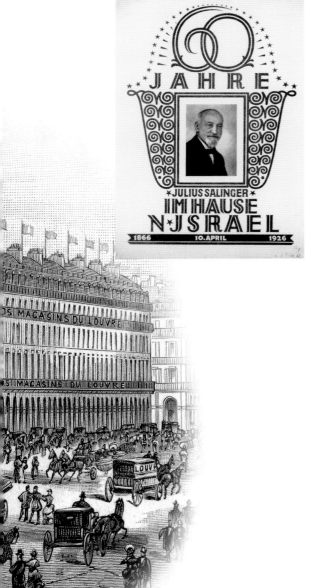

to do with its ability to create fashion. London might have excelled in quality goods and Philadelphia in utilitarian values, but Paris was queen of the style parade, and, just as it made an art of cooking and eating, it had a way of turning shopping into a sensory experience that laced a mundane chore with pleasure.

As much as they delighted and awed the public, department stores also had enemies, particularly during the economic depressions of the 1890s and 1930s. Opposition principally came from small tradespeople who felt threatened by the big stores' ability to afford huge advertising campaigns, corner the market in some goods, and undersell them. An estimated 7,500 small merchants had organized against department stores in Chicago by 1897.[9] Department stores were criticized for everything from forming buying cartels to running fraudulent advertising, selling shoddy goods, tempting women to shoplift, forcing low-paid women clerks into prostitution, and encouraging consumerism.[10] Special taxes were levied on them and restrictions were imposed on their operations in France, the United States, Germany, Japan, Switzerland, and Austria; they came in for criticism and ridicule everywhere.[11] A newspaper in one Western town in the United States tried to force consumers to shop locally by publishing a daily list of those who had ordered goods or shopped in department stores in a nearby city, though how they obtained this information is unknown.[12]

Catholic department-store owners in France, as well as New England Yankees and Protestants of all kinds in the U.S., were targeted—devout Protestant John Wanamaker even hired a bodyguard at one point—but Jewish owners suffered more attacks than others. In the U.S. there was little overt anti-Semitism, yet Leon Harris reports in *Merchant Princes* that the fear of anti-Semitism prevented many Jewish store owners from taking controversial stands on issues.[13] Anti-Semitism was severe in Germany, where the anti-department-store movement, which had begun in the late nineteenth century, merged with the National Socialist anti-Semitic currents of the 1920s and 1930s. A German critic wrote sneeringly in 1899 that the big stores sprang up like weeds: "One must observe how these uppity, self-aggrandizing grand bazaars and mass branch stores use their sensational marketing tactics to set themselves up everywhere..."[14] In the 1930s Nazi thugs started attacking stores, breaking windows, and harassing shoppers. Soon officials began enforced transfer of ownership to "Aryans." In Japan, too, the big department stores confronted opposition in the 1930s. They voluntarily halted expansion in 1932 in response to protests by small shopkeepers, though this did not prevent the passage of legal restrictions in 1937 that remained in force until 1947.[15]

BELLE JARDINIÈRE

LA MODE EN 1900

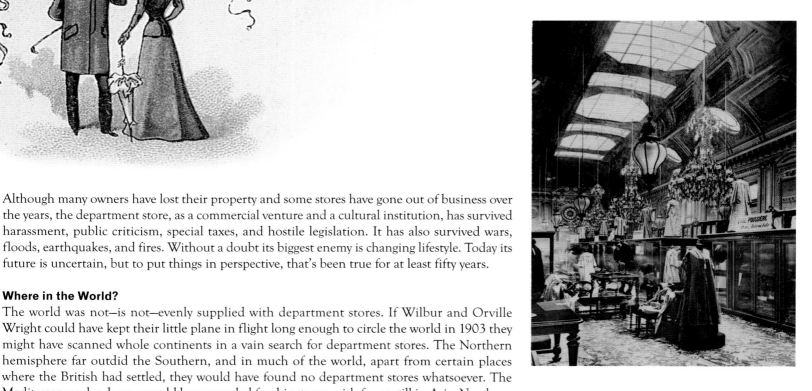

Although many owners have lost their property and some stores have gone out of business over the years, the department store, as a commercial venture and a cultural institution, has survived harassment, public criticism, special taxes, and hostile legislation. It has also survived wars, floods, earthquakes, and fires. Without a doubt its biggest enemy is changing lifestyle. Today its future is uncertain, but to put things in perspective, that's been true for at least fifty years.

Where in the World?

The world was not—is not—evenly supplied with department stores. If Wilbur and Orville Wright could have kept their little plane in flight long enough to circle the world in 1903 they might have scanned whole continents in a vain search for department stores. The Northern hemisphere far outdid the Southern, and in much of the world, apart from certain places where the British had settled, they would have found no department stores whatsoever. The Mediterranean landscape would have revealed few big stores, with fewer still in Asia. Northern Europe and Britain would have been more promising, especially Paris, where they would have spotted several stores with roofs large enough to land on, as an airplane would actually do some years later. Across the Atlantic and back in the United States, the numbers of store rooftops would have been plentiful as they flew over the Northeast, across the upper Midwest, and along the West Coast, but they would have found few large stores in the South.

France was still the unchallenged queen of department stores in 1903, but the United States was about to surpass her. Long before the Wright brothers' legendary adventure, as far back as 1874, Paris had been regarded as the best place for shopping in "the whole civilized world," a distinction the city held on to throughout the rest of the nineteenth century. Two names stood out among the dozen or so early stores that populated Paris, the Bon Marché and the Grands Magasins du Louvre, both of which came into prominence in the 1870s. These pioneering stores developed the world-standard formula and format for department stores. Among other features that were adopted, the name Bon Marché was borrowed by stores in Liverpool, Brussels, and as far away as the Congo and Washington state. Measured in volume of sales, the Bon Marché and the Louvre towered over their nearest competitors such as the Samaritaine and Printemps, doing more than three times as much business as the others at the end of the nineteenth century.[16] In addition to the big department stores, Paris was known for having many other large dry goods stores in the 1800s, such as Belle Jardinière, Bazar de l'Hôtel de Ville, Ville de St. Denis, Pygmalion, Petit Saint-Thomas, Tapis Rouge, and Magasins Dufayel.

CRESPIN

TAPIS MEUBLES LITERIE HORLOGERIE

BIJOUTERIE MIROITERIE LAMPES

The Bon Marché is widely credited with being the world's first department store, dating from 1852, when Aristide Boucicaut took command of the shop in which he worked. In the late 1860s he became the first to have a building designed and constructed specifically to house a department store; about the same time he expanded its stocks and implemented departmental organization.[17] Shortly after Boucicaut took over the Bon Marché, the Louvre opened. At first it occupied a portion of a hotel with the same name, but it wasn't long before it had bought out the hotel. The Bazar de l'Hôtel de Ville opened in 1860, followed five years later by Printemps, and then the Samaritaine a few years after that. In the 1870s the department store was fully developed in Paris, though store employees still numbered only in the hundreds.[18]

The Bon Marché remained one of the largest-volume department stores in the world well into the next century, but its competitors were growing stronger. Galeries Lafayette, one of the Paris stores that would come to prominence in the twentieth century and surpass the Bon Marché, was not founded until 1895. In 1911 the city's twelve largest department stores had a combined staff of 11,000, whereas the average small store had only about ten people.[19] Even by 1928 department-store development in Paris was still ahead of that in London and Berlin.[20] Several of Paris's big department stores began establishing branches in other French cities early in the twentieth century. In 1912 Printemps opened its first branch at Deauville. Over the next fifteen years it opened branches or subsidiaries in Le Havre, Rouen, and Lille. The Bon Marché opened its first branch in Vichy in 1918 and then in Reims, Roubaix, Toulouse, and Biarritz. In 1928 Galeries Lafayette owned a store in Lyons and, somewhat later, branches in Nice and Deauville.[21]

If Paris was the worldwide capital of department stores in the nineteenth century, the United States became its headquarters in the twentieth. Having more large cities than France, it also had more large stores. By 1919, according to retailing historian Paul Nystrom, there were about a hundred large department stores in the United States, as well as hundreds of smaller ones.[22] The origins of U.S. department stores can be traced as far back as their French counterparts'. A. T. Stewart, though primarily a wholesaler, also engaged in retailing, and in 1846 he created a "highly developed transition form" resembling a department store in New York City. In 1862 Stewart opened a large "palace" devoted to retail trade. Some consider him as much a creator of the department store as Aristide Boucicaut. Another contender for that honor is Rowland H. Macy, who around 1868 began to expand and diversify merchandise lines in his dry goods and fancy goods store on Sixth Avenue in Manhattan.[23]

OPPOSITE Fountain in the Siegel-Cooper store in New York City, ca. 1903. The statue is a replica of one by Daniel Chester French from the 1893 World's Columbian Exposition in Chicago. The store originated in Chicago and opened in New York's "Ladies Mile" shopping area in 1896.

ABOVE Occupying a city block, New York's Siegel-Cooper store faced the elevated train trestle on Sixth Avenue.

A handful of other American stores, whose descendants would one day expand the founder's business into a department store, opened in the 1840s, including the predecessors to G. Fox, Gimbels, and Joseph Horne in Pittsburgh. Others came later, such as Hutzler's, which opened as a dry goods store in Baltimore in 1858, and Mandel's, which began in Chicago in 1865. That was the same year that Marshall Field and Levi Leiter announced their partnership, and Wechsler & Abraham, forerunner to Abraham & Straus in Brooklyn, opened their doors. The 1840s and 1850s also marked the debuts of Lord & Taylor, Jordan Marsh, Lazarus, and Altman's as small dry goods stores.[24] Historian Paul Nystrom identifies the worldwide financial panic of 1873–74 as a major stimulant in the development of American department stores: as prices fell and many wholesalers and retailers went bankrupt, others took the opportunity to buy up their stocks and sell them as bargains.[25] Among the small stores founded in the 1870s that were destined for significant growth were The Fair in Chicago, L. S. Ayres in Indianapolis, Bloomingdale's in New York City, and Goldsmith's in Memphis. But the three stores that are considered America's first true, full-fledged department stores—all up and running by 1878—are Wanamaker's in Philadelphia, Macy's in New York, and Jordan Marsh in Boston.[26]

Another store that has laid claim to being America's first has distinctive characteristics that point to differences among Eastern and Western U.S. stores in the formative years. Nothing could be further from the origins or development of the Bon Marché, for instance, than Zion's Cooperative Mercantile Institution (ZCMI) of Salt Lake City. Established in 1868, when Salt Lake City's population was less than 13,000, ZCMI carried covered wagons, machinery of various kinds, and hardware needed by pioneers in a new settlement, as well as food supplies and work clothes. Given its outpost location, the basic supplies it furnished, and its lack of the fashion component usually considered a requisite of department stores, it might better be thought of as an enlarged general store in its early years, but it illustrates a settlement type of department store.

The 1890s saw the appearance of major American stores such as Bamberger's in Newark, Siegel-Cooper in Chicago and New York City, Bonwit Teller and Wanamaker's in New York City, Bon Marché and Frederick & Nelson in Seattle, The Emporium in San Francisco, Lit Brothers and Gimbels in Philadelphia, and Woodward & Lothrop in Washington, D.C. Marshall Field, at the conclusion of its huge building program from 1892 to 1907, became the world's largest store in area (1.5 million square feet) and the nation's largest in sales volume, ranking just below the Bon Marché and the Grands Magasins du Louvre in Paris.[27]

As the twentieth century dawned, many stores were just getting their start in what has been called the "golden years" of American department-store growth.[28] Among them were Dayton's in Minneapolis, Gimbels in New York City, Bullocks in Los Angeles, and major women's specialty stores like Bergdorf Goodman, Franklin Simon, Neiman Marcus, and Saks Fifth Avenue. In 1900 there were about ten large department stores in Boston, among them Filene's, Jordan Marsh, R. H. White, Gilchrist's, R. H. Stearns, and Shepards. Nonetheless, Chicago and Philadelphia were no doubt America's premier department-store cities in the first decade of the century. New York was well supplied with oversized emporiums, but because of its greater population and drawing power for outlying shoppers, it tended to have many more large specialty stores than smaller cities, and consequently department stores dominated retailing to a far lesser extent there than elsewhere.[29] In the 1920s Gimbels and Franklin Simon, as well as older New York City stores such as Macy's, Altman's, and Lord & Taylor were counted among the world's largest stores in volume of sales, as were Wanamaker's, Lit's, and Snellenburg's in Philadelphia, the last estimated by the *Wall Street Journal* to be on an equal footing then with the Bon Marché in Paris.[30] The early twentieth century also witnessed the spread of department stores into smaller towns across the United States.[31]

Outside the United States department stores captured a far smaller share of the retailing market than might be popularly thought. According to 1928 calculations, American department stores took the greatest market share of any country, 16 percent. Next in line was Holland with 8 percent, then France with 5.3–6.3 percent, followed either by Germany with a 4 percent share or Great Britain with 3.5–4.5 percent. In Sweden the department store market share was only 1.8 percent; in Spain it was lower still.[32]

After the world wars, urban traffic congestion, combined with the growth of suburbia and the competition of specialty stores and low-price chains, led department stores to move closer to where their affluent customers lived. In the words of consumer consultant Christine Frederick, "Traffic conditions in large cities point clearly to a decentralizing tendency, and as a consumer I loudly applaud."[33] Stores in New York City, Chicago, Philadelphia, St. Louis, Cleveland, and Detroit were eager to branch out. Marshall Field built substantial branch stores in Evanston, Lake Forest, and Oak Park, Illinois, in the 1920s. B. Altman opened a store in White Plains, New York, Filene's in Worcester, Massachusetts, and Strawbridge & Clothier opened its first branch in 1929 in Ardmore, Pennsylvania. Branching intensified in the 1950s with the construction of suburban shopping centers, and by the 1960s the larger stores tended to have ten or so outlets, which collectively did a greater business than the flagship.[34]

Visible beyond the Sixth Avenue elevated train is Saks 34th Street, and past it is a glimpse of Macy's at Herald Square.

Stairway in rotunda of Wanamaker's, New York City, originally the A. T. Stewart store.

Department stores in England had a slow start because of cultural factors that encouraged conservative business practices. Many of the shops that eventually became department stores dated back to the early nineteenth century. Dickins & Jones, Swan & Edgar, Debenhams, and James Shoolbred & Co. originated before the 1830s as dry goods stores—"drapers" in England.[35] Their growth was also slow. As historian John William Ferry wrote, "At the mid-century, London had nothing to compare with A. T. Stewart's Marble Palace of 1848, or his Manhattan department store erected fourteen years later."[36] Not until the 1860s and 1870s did the English department store begin to emerge with various lines of merchandise brought together under one roof; they did not become sizable until the 1890s.[37]

In the 1860s and 1870s, the growth and development of English department stores was simultaneously hampered and stimulated by competition from cooperative stores, which were established by and for the middle classes to reduce the cost of retail goods.[38] The Civil Service Cooperative Society and the Army and Navy Cooperative Society operated no-frills stores with few services. Somewhat like the government stores that would be organized in the 1920s in the Soviet Union, co-op shoppers had to fill out requests for merchandise, which was later sent to their homes. Although they lacked certain essential features of department stores such as the evocation of desire through elaborate displays, luxurious interiors, and royal treatment of shoppers, co-ops shared such principles as fixed prices, high turnover, and low prices. These characteristics, along with cash sales and direct buying from manufacturers without the aid of middlemen, are thought to have preceded the diversification of merchandise by businesses that would grow into department stores.[39]

In 1849 Harrods was still a small grocer. Its transformation into a department store occurred under the impetus of the cooperative stores. In 1868 it added perfumes, patent medicines, and stationery to its stocks, and imitated the co-ops by issuing a price list,[40] but by 1880 it still had only 150 employees. Upon incorporation in 1889 it started growing rapidly, although, like Whiteleys and Lewis's, which were undergoing similar processes, its growth was slower than that of stores in France or the United States.[41] Even in the 1890s Whiteleys and Harrods consisted of "little more than terraces of interconnected shops,"[42] but their business volume was becoming sizable. Whiteleys employed a staff of nearly five thousand in the late 1880s. By the mid-1890s it was considered one of the world's great stores, ranking in volume just behind the top three: the Bon Marché and the Grands Magasins du Louvre in Paris and Marshall Field in Chicago.[43] It was London's best-known store in the late nineteenth century.

Harrods and Whiteleys were London's largest department stores when Harry Gordon Selfridge came to the city in 1909 and opened a store based on American retailing methods, which included massive advertising. He regarded his competitors as old-fashioned and hoped to outdo them. In 1927 Selfridges absorbed Whiteleys in hopes of surpassing sales at Harrods. Although this acquisition may have boosted Selfridges' position briefly, it did not succeed in dislodging Harrods as London's leading store.[44] As was true elsewhere, the largest department stores in England were those that developed into chains. By 1931 not only had Whiteleys been absorbed but another of the pioneers, Shoolbred's, was gone entirely. The survivors such as Harrods, Selfridges, and a few others expanded rapidly, opened branches, and acquired existing stores, a process that in more recent years has produced major chains such as John Lewis and Debenham's.

Like England, Germany was a nation of small shopkeepers and conservative business methods. Until near the end of the nineteenth century, German department stores were small and located primarily in towns of less than 50,000. Wertheim, which Berliners would call their Bon Marché in the early 1900s, opened its first two stores in Stralsund in 1876 and 1880 and a third in Rostock in 1884. Leonhard Tietz founded his first store, which sold fabric and tailoring supplies, in Stralsund in 1879. His uncle Hermann Tietz opened stores in Gera in 1882, Weimar in 1886, and Munich in 1889.[45] Karstadt began in Wismar in 1881.[46]

German cities began a mighty growth spurt toward the end of the nineteenth century, and in the 1890s the department-store scene in Germany began to resemble that in other countries where the big stores have flourished. Karstadt began to open stores in Hamburg; Leonhard Tietz, in Cologne, Aachen, Mainz, and Düsseldorf, among others; Schmoller, in Frankfurt; and Hermann Tietz, in Hamburg and Berlin. Wertheim entered Berlin, where it would open its massive Leipziger Strasse store in 1896.[47]

By 1907 there were about two hundred department stores in Germany, and by the start of World War I the number had doubled.[48] In Berlin, many were housed in new and imposing buildings designed by the country's leading architects. Wertheim's five large Berlin stores dominated the cityscape, and Hermann Tietz had three stores in the center of Berlin, with its Leipziger Strasse store next door to Wertheim. The Kaufhaus des Westens (KaDeWe), completed in 1907, was the seventh Berlin store of Hamburg wholesaler Jandorf, which established its first Berlin store in 1892.[49] The elegant Nathan Israel department store, which was founded as a dry goods store in 1815, developed into a department store with two thousand employees in the twentieth century and earned a reputation for quality that some felt rivaled Harrods in London.[50]

KAKTEEN   KAKTEEN

Many large stores were located in other German cities. Frankfurt was the home of Wronker and Schmoller; Hamburg, of Karstadt; Leipzig and Essen, of Althoff. Munich had a store owned by Hermann Tietz. In 1901 Salman Schocken and his brother Simon founded their first department store in Zwickau, launching a business that would grow to a chain of twenty stores by the time the company was taken over under the Nazis in the 1930s.[51] Leonhard Tietz, headquartered in Cologne after 1891, controlled eighteen department stores in Germany and four in Belgium by 1907. Overall, just before the Nazi ascent to power, Germany was about equal to England in the development of department stores.[52] In 1929 the largest German firms were Karstadt, Tietz, Wertheim, and Schocken, in that order.

By 1930 Karstadt was not just Germany's largest department-store chain, but with 89 stores, 27 factories, and over 29,000 employees, it was also Europe's largest department-store concern.[53] It was corporate owned from the start, with both Jewish and non-Jewish owners, the principal founder being Rudolf Karstadt, who was not Jewish. The store received a major loan approved by Hitler's Cabinet in 1933, negotiated by two executives who belonged to the National Socialist party, while Karstadt was undergoing voluntary Aryanization. Each issue of the store's newsletter at this time featured a quotation from Hitler. After the war, the store began making restitution for its program of "self-Aryanization," and went on to become Europe's largest department-store company.[54]

Although the same might be said of each nation, the course of department stores in Japan is unique. The country was late to establish a department-store culture, but when it did it presented the world with some of its most celebrated stores. Many, such as Mitsukoshi, Shirokiya, Takashimaya, and Daimaru, developed out of seventeenth-century dry goods stores. Although major department stores did not become firmly established in Japan until after its recovery from World War II, once they did take hold, the task was accomplished with enormous flair. By the early 1950s four Japanese stores—Daimaru, Matsuzakaya, Mitsukoshi, and Takashimaya, in that order—had achieved significant size.[55] A few years later, the Japan Department Store Association reported that there were about eighty large department stores in the country, not counting branches. Subsequent years saw the rise of department stores in shopping complexes situated at major commuter railway stops such as Shinjuku, Shibuya, and Ikebukuro. Most of these began as purely utilitarian shopping depots, but some gradually changed to resemble the industry leaders. Seibu, in particular, remade itself into a fashionable, trend-setting store in the 1970s, installing an art museum in its Ikebukuro branch. For the greatest part of Japan's department-store history, however, Mitsukoshi held the top spot.

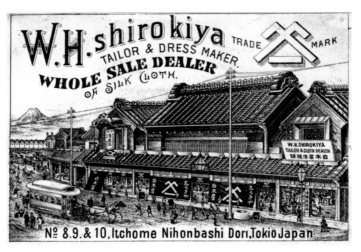

In some countries, such as Canada and Australia, mail order played a particularly large role in store development. Mail-order business was important for department stores all over the world, especially before World War II, but it assumed greater proportions in places where the population was spread thinly and low parcel-post rates facilitated sending packages long distances. Simpson's and Eaton's attained full-fledged department-store status in Toronto in the 1890s. Though still relatively small, the Robert Simpson Company had a massive mail-order department; the T. Eaton Company, a larger business with five times as many employees in the late 1890s, ran a highly profitable mail-order operation as well. Eaton's was the country's largest retailer by 1905 and had opened a second big store and factories in Winnipeg. The store rivaled Marshall Field in the United States and did a greater business than Macy's or Harrods at that time, though by World War I it had been surpassed by Whiteleys and Selfridges in London. The Hudson's Bay Company stores, founded as British fur-trading posts in the seventeenth century, became department stores in western Canada in the first couple of decades of the twentieth century, a bit later than Woodward's in Vancouver was incorporated.[56] In 1922 HBC had eleven stores.

Spring and Summer mail-order catalog of Myer's department store in Melbourne, 1906–7.

Of the three earliest department stores in Sydney, Australia, all having forerunners dating back to the mid-nineteenth century, only one, David Jones, survived beyond the 1970s. Of the other two, Anthony Hordern closed in the 1970s and Farmer's merged with the Myer Emporium in 1960. The real development of Australian department stores didn't get under way until the early twentieth century. Hordern's, begun as a millinery shop, had enlarged into a universal provider in the 1880s, selling "all things needful, and everything nice," but became a significant retailer only about 1905.[57] David Jones became a public company in 1906 and its main store at Elizabeth and Market streets opened in 1927.[58] Sidney Myer opened his store in Melbourne in 1911, launching what would become the largest chain of department stores in Australia.

In other parts of the globe where the British and Europeans created settlements, department stores took hold to a certain degree. In South Africa, for instance, there were notable department stores in Cape Town, Durban, and Johannesburg, appearing—with few exceptions such as Payne Brothers in Durban—somewhat later than in Australia and Canada.[59]

Until the state took over department-store operations following the Bolshevik revolution in 1917, Moscow's only significant department store was Muir & Mirrielees, a British-run store established in the 1880s. Among the largest of the state-run stores established in the early 1920s were GUM (State Universal Store) and TsUM (Central Universal Store) in Moscow and smaller stores in Leningrad. Until the fall of Communism, however, these stores, though in-

CATALOGUE N°62

Spring & Summer

1899

The Robert SIMPSON Co. Limited.

TORONTO, CANADA.

PRECEDING PAGES
Serving as a quasi-department store in the Soviet era, today Moscow's GUM has returned to its original 1893 function as an arcade of small shops.

INSET The GUM trademark, "GUM 1893 Red Square."

BELOW Transverse passage crossing the three GUM galleries.

ABOVE In the 1930s, workers wash one of GUM's glass roofs. In the background is a recently built Stalinist skyscraper.

RIGHT The clock and watch shop of the Kalashnikov brothers at the 1893 opening of the complex that would become GUM after the Bolshevik revolution.

OPPOSITE Contemporary café in the GUM mall. The complex has become far more elegant since the fall of Communism.

tended as mechanisms for mass distribution, were not run in a way comparable to department
stores in capitalist countries. There was little merchandise on display and consumers were not
free to browse. They were required to place an order at a central desk and then pick up their
purchase after paying at another station.[60]

In the Low Countries, Scandinavia, and Switzerland, department-store development, involving
such stores as Magazine zum Globus in Switzerland, L'Innovation in Belgium, and de Bijenkorf
in Holland, started around 1890. The Magasijn de Bijenkorf grew out of a dry goods store
begun in the 1870s by Simon Philip Goudsmit. Under the direction of his heirs, it developed
into a department store via financing connections supplied by Germany's Tietz stores.[61]
Copenhagen's Magasin du Nord had begun to resemble a department store a decade earlier.[62]
Like the Grands Magasins du Louvre in Paris, it had its start occupying the lower floors of a
hotel, in this case a hotel with a reputation, known as the "Bordel du Nord." After making a
good profit from visitors to Copenhagen's 1888 world's fair, the store bought the hotel, tore
it down, and built a new headquarters.[63] Stockholm's Nordiska Kompaniet (also known as
N.K.), Scandinavia's largest department store, was founded in 1902 through the merger of two
earlier stores. Other major Scandinavian stores include Oslo's Steen & Strøm and Helsinki's
Stockmann.

Eastern Europe and the Mediterranean countries did not witness early or extensive development of large department stores, although several prominent chains arose later in the twentieth century such as El Corte Inglés in Spain (originally a tailor shop established in 1934) and
La Rinascente in Italy. It is striking that the department store has played such a small role in
Rome despite its status as a major global city, reconfirming that the development of big stores
has been more dependent on the degree of industrialization and the prominence and wealth
of the middle class than on the size of urban areas.[64] La Rinascente began in 1889 when
Ferdinando Bocconi and his brother opened a store in the style of Paris's Bon Marché on the
Piazza Duomo in Milan. By 1900 there were branches in Venice, Florence, Turin, Genoa,
Naples, Bologna, and Palermo. Financial difficulties during World War I led Bocconi to sell
the store, whereupon the new owner renamed it La Rinascente ("Born Again") to commemo-
rate its rebirth. The Depression devastated the chain; twelve of its seventeen stores closed, although the company's chain of variety stores, run under the name UPIM, grew.[65]

The creation of branches outside the country of origin was led by a Parisian store, the Samaritaine,
which opened a London store as early as 1902, though it was not successful and closed after World

LEFT Men's hats, at
Stockmann in
Helsinki, 1932.

ABOVE First floor in
Oslo's Steen & Strøm,
ca. 1920.

War I. Harrods branched into Argentina, which it considered "the United States of the Southern Hemisphere," in 1913, while the Bon Marché, Printemps, and Galeries Lafayette had agencies, presumably for mail orders, in Peru by 1920, about which time the Bon Marché was planning a store in Algiers. In Mexico City, the Palacio de Hierro and El Centro Mercantil, both designed by French architects, brought fin de siècle elegance to the Mexican capital. Nordiska Kompaniet had stores in Buenos Aires, Petrograd, and Moscow by 1921. In the 1930s Galeries Lafayette would also have stores in Brussels, Bucharest, and Rome. Japan's Seibu opened an ill-fated branch in Los Angeles in 1962, as did Printemps with a franchise store in Denver in the 1980s. Printemps also had franchise stores in Japan, Saudi Arabia, Finland, Malaysia, and Turkey, and opened shops on the ocean liners *L'Atlantique* in 1932 and *France* in 1962. Whereas American department stores confined their branches to the national borders, the branching and franchising operations of companies such as Debenhams, Mitsukoshi, Takashimaya, Seibu, and others have enabled the spread of department stores throughout the world.

Who in the World?

Department stores were many things—architectural structures, sets of retail practices, and collections of merchandise—but it was people who made them work. They could not have existed without shoppers, clerks, and delivery van drivers, but it was often founders or business families who gave them their character and who made them icons of their cities, regions, or countries.

Reflecting their self-creation as myths, their leading role in the developing field of public relations, and the public's readiness to turn them into the stuff of legend, department stores often emphasize their humble origins—a tiny shop, a poor peddler—ignoring the need of large-scale retailers to amass capital, usually from financial institutions. But if the rags-to-riches stories have been overplayed in commemorative histories, it is true that despite many owners' wishes to remain private, founders' names have over time attained stature extending far beyond the realm of commerce.

It was said of French department-store magnates that they became known only when they died and left behind a fortune and an impressive art collection. This statement could apply to the founders and owners of stores in many other countries as well. To the general public, most of the men who founded department stores were ciphers during their lifetimes. Their names might be famous, but little of substance was actually known about them. The public had never seen them and they remained little more than symbols of a type—the rich and successful busi-

nessman. What was said of Alexander Turney Stewart was true of most: although Stewart's name was recognized around the world, during his lifetime he was perceived as "a myth, with no personal entity."[66]

If a motto could reveal the soul of department-store founders, it would be Harry Gordon Selfridge's "There's no fun like work."[67] The typical founder was someone who came from a humble background and made his way through hard work, beginning in his teens. He, or occasionally she, was unfamiliar with leisure and luxury and sometimes continued to live humbly despite the acquisition of a fortune. Ernest and Louise Cognacq practically lived at the Samaritaine, the Paris department store they founded. It was said that they never took a holiday in fifty years of running the store together and that on the one occasion they had planned a getaway they canceled it at the last minute. Each morning, until Mme. Cognacq became infirm, they rode a bus to the store, returning home late in the evening. They spent their Sundays going over the books and viewing the new week's window displays.[68] New York's A. T. Stewart, known for being "a slave to business," worked eight to ten hours a day well into his sixties, despite having amassed a fortune second only to William B. Astor's.[69] Even in old age founders couldn't drag themselves out of the store, not recognizing in some cases that they had lost their grip.

Most of the people who founded and ran department stores preferred to stay out of the limelight. The Cognacqs of the Samaritaine, the Boucicauts of the Bon Marché, Benjamin Altman, and Marshall Field were all modest, retiring people who avoided publicity. Few knew what bachelor Altman looked like. Marshall Field refused to take the proffered role of Chicago's sage, requesting the press to leave him alone.

In a sense they were all outsiders, lacking power, capital, or social connections; this was especially true for Jewish store founders, many of whom faced hostility and close scrutiny from officials and commercial competitors. Jewish owners were most numerous in the United States and in Germany, although the founders of the Galeries Lafayette in Paris, De Bijenkorf in Holland, and L'Innovation in Brussels were Jews, as was David Lewis, whose small Liverpool shop would turn into a string of moderate-priced provincial English department stores. German Jews such as Salman Schocken and members of the Tietz and Wertheim families experienced the extremes of ostracism with the Nazi takeover of their stores in the 1930s. An outsider of a different sort was Tsutsumi Seiji, manager of Seibu in Japan. As one of the illegitimate sons of magnate Tsutsumi Yasujiro, he faced rejection by schoolmates as well as a difficult relationship with his father.[70]

Department-store founders, owners, and managers represented a variety of religions and ethnicities, from the Quakers of Strawbridge and Clothier of Philadelphia to Catholics in France. German Jews, such as the Gimbels, Foxes, Filenes, and the Straus family of Macy's, were prominent in American large-scale retailing, as they were in Germany. The Carsons and Piries of Carson Pirie Scott and the founders of Rochester's Sibley, Lindsay & Curr represent only a few of the Protestant Scotsmen who came into department stores via the dry goods trade. Catholic founders, however, were rare in the department-store industry of the United States, as were Italians, Asians, Greeks, Irish, and Eastern Europeans.

Having many male offspring was key to keeping a store under family control, as the history of the Gimbels and Strauses illustrates. Adam Gimbel had seven sons, who presided over the store's expansion into several American cities beyond its initial site, Milwaukee. A Straus remained at the helm of Macy's until 1968, when Jack Straus retired as chairman. Lacking a son, Moses Fox handed over control of his store in Hartford, Connecticut, to his daughter, Beatrice Fox Auerbach, but this was highly unusual. A surprising number of founders had no children or lost them at a young age, including A. T. Stewart, Benjamin Altman, Alfred Chauchard, the Boucicauts, and Marshall Field. John Wanamaker lost his son Thomas as he was being groomed to run the Philadelphia store, while his son Rodman, head of the New York store, died not long after his father in the 1920s.

Over the long run an exclusively family-owned store was a shaky proposition. Many stores passed into corporate ownership after the founder died, while others started out as corporate enterprises. The Emporium of San Francisco was not the only store that developed out of real estate speculation in the 1890s and early 1900s. In the case of Japan's Mitsukoshi, the "family" was a trust comprised of many families who together ran one of the world's largest companies. The House of Mitsui not only had mercantile interests but controlled much of the banking and mining industries in Japan. In 1910 it had bank branches all over Japan, six coal mines employing 10,000 miners, and silver, lead, and zinc mines. It was also the financial agent for the Mikado theater company, was reputed to have financed the Russo-Japanese War, and at times controlled as much as one-seventh of Japan's foreign trade.[71] In France, a family of sorts was created by setting up an employee ruling council and giving council members bequests and financial stakes in the store. This structure kept the Bon Marché from becoming a public corporation after the Boucicauts were gone, whereas the Grands Magasins du Louvre became a public company in 1890 and the Samaritaine in 1914.[72] Ownership and control of German

LEFT Nazi storm troopers in front of the N. Israel store in Berlin announce a boycott of Jewish-owned stores, 1933. Two years later the store was appropriated from its owners and "Aryanized."

ABOVE Isidor Straus, head of Macy's and part owner of Brooklyn's Abraham & Straus, was a German-Jewish American who came to New York after the Civil War to help his father set up a crockery and glassware business. In 1896 he and his brother Nathan became owners of the store founded by R. H. Macy, where they had once managed a crockery and glass department. Isidor and his wife perished on the *Titanic* in 1912.

stores was shifted from Jews to "Aryans" after the National Socialists came to power in the 1930s; Jewish store owners, managers, and workers were forced out and replaced. The Tietz family, owner of the Hermann Tietz stores, survived attacks from Socialists following World War I and then takeover attempts by non-family senior executives, only to fall to the Nazis in 1934.[73] Whatever their background, and despite the lack of much formal education, many department store founders exhibited early signs of business acumen. Marshall Field revealed mercantile instincts as a schoolboy trading jackknives, and John Wanamaker published a magazine in his teens. Stewart seemed to have had little identity outside of business. It was said of him that he "thinks money, makes money, lives money" and that "his soul was in bargains."[74] As other merchants succumbed to pre-Civil War panic, he continued buying and selling. In the process, he gained control of the cotton market and emerged after the war enormously richer. "If he was a prince before the war," it was said, "he . . . was a king after it."[75]

Many department-store founders had business involvements beyond their stores that accounted for a portion of their fortunes. Both Stewart and Field were heavily invested in real estate. Field owned much of Chicago's State Street and held shares in railroads, mines, steel, and the Pullman railway car company.[76] Stewart had properties in New York City and owned the Grand Union Hotel in Saratoga and an estate at Hempstead Plains on Long Island, which was destined to become the town of Garden City.[77] Germany's Hermann Wronker co-founded a film company that later became the legendary UFA studio.[78] Salman Schocken began publishing in Germany, later transferring his operations to Tel Aviv and then the United States in 1945, when he founded Schocken Books, publisher of the works of Franz Kafka and other world-renowned authors.[79] Jules Jaluzot of Printemps, owner of a sugar refinery at Origny-Sainte-Benoite, enjoyed great financial success as a speculator for a time but eventually brought about his own downfall by cornering the sugar market, which then collapsed and created a worldwide financial panic.[80]

Department-store founders and their successors figured prominently in the art world, both as collectors and sometimes as creators. Then, as now, it was de rigueur for a wealthy man to collect art, thus explaining why even department-store owners such as the Cognacqs or A. T. Stewart—whose artistic sensibilities were not highly cultivated—amassed collections. Meissonier's *Friedland, 1807* from Stewart's collection eventually made its way into the Metropolitan Museum of Art. The museum was also the recipient of Benjamin Altman's valuable collection. Against the advice of the modernist architect of their store, Ernest and Louise

OPPOSITE A room in the Cognacq-Jay Museum, donated to Paris by the founders of the Samaritaine, Ernest and Louise Cognacq.

BELOW Jules Jaluzot, founder of Printemps, began his department-store career as a clerk at the Bon Marché.

Cognacq sold off their collection of Impressionist paintings to focus on eighteenth-century art. They enshrined their collection in a museum they built next to the store, the Cognacq-Jay, which they eventually bequeathed to the city of Paris. The collection of Grands Magasins du Louvre founder Alfred Chauchard included several Millets, among them the artist's most famous work, *The Angelus*. Chauchard also owned paintings by Meissonier and Corot, and a fabulously expensive Gobelin carpet on which he allowed no one to step but himself. In 1910 the first floor of the Pavillon de Flore at the Louvre Museum held 140 of his paintings.[81] Schocken focused on literature, amassing a collection that consisted of rare manuscripts as well as over 60,000 volumes of Jewish and world literature.

Tsutsumi Seiji of Seibu and Charles Lloyd Jones, grandson of founder David Jones of Sydney's store of that name, were producers as well as patrons of the arts. Tsutsumi was a poet and the author of two novels, while Jones's paintings hung in the National Art Gallery in Sydney and the Melbourne Art Gallery. Jones also founded the publication *Art in Australia*, supported the theater and symphony, and was chairman of the first Australian Broadcasting Commission.[82]

Being the founder of a department store often carried with it a high degree of community respect. In the words of Leon Harris, mayors might be corrupt or forgettable, "But 'Mr. Goldsmith' in Memphis or 'Mr. Thalhimer' in Richmond, 'Mr. Halle' in Cleveland or 'Mr. Weinstock' in Sacramento was known to virtually every citizen in his community..."[83] When a founder died, not only would the store close down on the day of the funeral, but in many cases the whole city took note and sometimes much of the business of the city halted as well. The mayor of Cleveland ordered flags flown at half-mast on public buildings when Sam Halle of Halle's died. John Wanamaker's rites gave public schools half a day off, closed the stock exchange, the city council, and all of Philadelphia's department stores. Marshall Field's funeral occasioned closure of the Chicago stock exchange for half a day. Paris mourned for Mme. Boucicaut and Mme. Cognacq, though, characteristically, Louise Cognacq had requested that the store remain open during her funeral.[84]

Public respect for a department store magnate was not automatic and could be forfeited through bad deeds. Although Alfred Chauchard had intended to provide for retired employees of the Louvre with land in a village near Versailles to be named Chauchardville, the plan was never realized and his will left little to charitable causes.[85] During the elaborate funeral parade that he had so carefully planned and that drew half a million viewers, cars in the cortege were attacked by the crowd, who threw flowers from his bier about the street. Many hissed as

RIGHT Timothy Eaton, founder of Eaton's department store, with his son and successor, John Craig Eaton, 1899. The Eatons were often referred to as the second royal family in Canada.

the body passed and the tone of the whole event was more carnival than funeral, perhaps revealing the French public's high expectations of philanthropy from wealthy department-store owners.[86] A few department-store magnates were gamblers and playboys, and at least a couple were involved in serious criminal activities. Henry Siegel and Jules Jaluzot both succumbed to raiding depositors' accounts in their stores' banks when they were in desperate need of funds due to unwise business ventures.[87] William Whiteley, like Selfridge a reputed womanizer, met his end at the hands of his illegitimate son.[88]

Chauchard's stinginess may have been an exception, for philanthropy was commonplace among store owners. As Scrooge-like as he could be about business, A. T. Stewart was also extremely generous. He bought a ship, filled it with provisions, and sent it to Ireland during the famine of the 1840s. For its return trip he solicited young Irish men and women passengers and had jobs waiting for them upon landing in New York. He donated $100,000 to the Union Army's Sanitary Commission during the Civil War and sent a ship loaded with flour to avert famine in Paris at the end of the Franco-Prussian war. After the fire that virtually destroyed Chicago in 1871 he donated $50,000 to that city's relief efforts.[89] Former organizer for the YMCA and Sunday school founder Wanamaker established a citizens' committee for nationwide famine, flood, and epidemic relief.[90] The Cognacqs were awarded a ribbon of the French Legion of Honor for an endowment fund that made bequests to large families. Mme. Cognacq's special project was building and endowing a maternity home for impoverished women.[91] Marshall Field donated $1 million for Chicago's natural history museum, and Eben Jordan gave Boston an opera house.[92] Macy's Straus family engaged in many philanthropies, but Nathan Straus in particular devoted much of his life and fortune to activities such as providing pasteurized milk to children, assisting war orphans, and helping to establish the state of Israel.[93]

When reclusive bachelor Benjamin Altman died in 1913, he left nearly his entire $50 million fortune to the public and to his store employees. About $30 million was dedicated to creating a profit-sharing fund for workers at the Fifth Avenue store, while his immensely valuable art collection went to New York's Metropolitan Museum of Art. In light of the importance of the collection in building the museum's stature, it was recognized then as "the greatest gift ever given to this museum." Although Altman had started collecting Chinese vases in the 1880s, he began to acquire paintings in 1905 expressly for the purpose of bequeathing them. In addition to over five hundred pieces of Chinese porcelain, his collection contained hundreds of sculptures, fifty European paintings, including thirteen Rembrandts, and many other notable works.

Oskar Tietz and his uncle Hermann Tietz supported Jewish projects financially and aided Jewish refugees of Russian pogroms in 1903 and 1905, helping them to obtain German residence permits or emigrate to America. The Tietz family was also closely involved with the German state during World War I. The military commandeered equipment from them, including delivery trucks and a personal yacht, and Oskar Tietz was a delegate of the Red Cross while his son Georg was associated with "cultural propaganda" for the War Ministry. In this role Georg raised funds for German prisoners of war interned in Switzerland by organizing them to produce handicrafts that were then sold in the Tietz department stores. However, his services did not prevent him from being recalled to arms in an anti-Semitic military draft that called up Jews before all others.[94]

Honors were heaped on department-store leaders. In countries affiliated with Britain, a sense of royalty attached to public service. In Canada, the Eatons were known as "Canada's Royal Family." John Craig Eaton, son of the founder, was knighted in 1915 for service to the Commonwealth, including the donation of $100,000 to equip a military outfit, as well as offering his private yacht and his wireless station to the government for the war effort.[95] In London, Richard Burbidge, once a manager at Whiteleys and named head of Harrods in 1893, was made a baronet in 1916 for his services to the government during the war. He served on committees to organize canteens, an aircraft factory, and other needs, and he made a large anonymous donation to preserve the Crystal Palace. In recognition of his influence and advice in financial matters, Hachiroemon Mitsui, head of the House of Mitsui, was made a peer.[96] Others held high office or, in the case of Stewart, almost did. He was chosen by President U.S. Grant to be his secretary of the treasury but failed to get confirmation from the Senate because of a conflict of interest concerning import tariffs. Wanamaker served as postmaster general from 1889 to 1893 and ran as a Republican for various offices, none of which he won. London's J. Barker was a member of Parliament in the early twentieth century; Jesse Straus was appointed ambassador to France by President Franklin Roosevelt; and Jules Jaluzot had been a member of the Chamber of Deputies before his fall from grace.[97]

The Endless Shopping Spree

Department stores may not be able to take all the credit for inventing modern shopping, but they certainly made its conventions and conveniences commonplace. They set a new standard for the way the consumer should expect to be treated, the type of services that should be provided for free or at minimal cost, and the convenience that should attend the process of acquiring the necessities and niceties of life all in one place. In short, they made shopping into a leisure pastime.

Before Department Stores

One of the shopping conventions most often cited as an innovation of department stores was the practice of marking prices on goods, thus preventing clerks from quoting different prices to customers based on their presumed ability to pay and degree of skill at haggling.[1] Before department stores came on the scene, clerks had the upper hand in the haggling system, for only they possessed knowledge of the true bottom price that the store would accept. Although the practice of determining price by haggling, commonly known as "cheapening," was starting to disappear as early as the 1830s, it was still common in many places when proto–department stores began to emerge in the late 1850s.[2] It seems to have been especially entrenched in the smaller shops in London, about which a veteran shopper remarked, "A shopping expedition in London is not a pleasant operation..."[3]

According to shoppers, clerks often misunderstood customers' wants, took up their time, and harangued and insulted them if they bought too little or dared not to buy anything. Once a shopper entered a store, she was expected to go straight to the relevant counter and not leave the store without having made a purchase. After the sale, however, she was expected to go away. Looking around freely was not permitted, as Harry Gordon Selfridge learned on a scouting expedition to London before he built his store there. When he tried to browse in one London store, a floorwalker became suspicious of his intentions and rudely told him to "[H]op it."[4]

All in all, tension and mistrust characterized the relationship between customers and store personnel. The slowness and unpleasantness of shopping, along with the difficulty of seeing and touching the goods, clogged the "pipeline" that was to carry the fruits of mass production to the burgeoning mass of consumers, money in hand yet unable to make purchases quickly and easily. In addition, the traditional customs of a neighborhood-based system of small shops that tacitly agreed not to advertise or lower prices because competition meant unfairly "stealing" business from their neighbors provided further restrictions on the development of trade. The

PRECEDING PAGES
LEFT Cover of Printemps rug catalog, 1920.
RIGHT Detail of Bon Marché publicity piece, 1900.

OPPOSITE Imaginary reconstruction of an impossibly fabric-laden scene in a silk department of an 1860s Paris store. Almost certainly, this is a still from the 1943 film *Au Bonheur des dames*, later retitled *The Shop Girls of Paris*.

ABOVE French saleswoman arranging a display of fabrics. Despite this image, before the arrival of department stores, most salesclerks were male.

RIGHT Scene in the receiving department of a Paris shop of the 1830s.

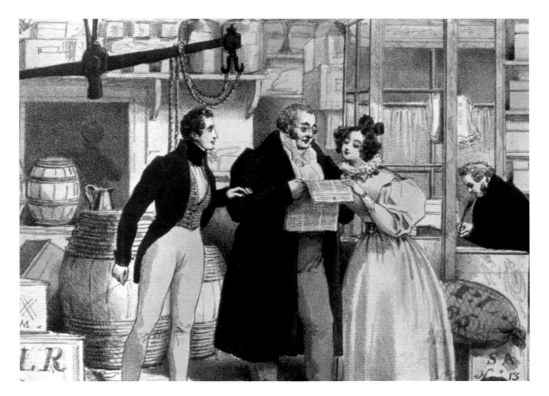

old system was codified in an eighteenth-century ordinance in France that prohibited merchants from undercutting each other with low prices "and particularly prohibited the distribution of advertising leaflets to promote their wares."[5] It took a long time for the effects of this well-entrenched system to disappear.

The convenience of shopping for a variety of articles under one roof, as in a department store, seems like an obvious kind of innovation until one sees it in the context of the incredibly high degree of merchandise specialization that long prevailed in large cities. In sum, the before-department-store customer, particularly if he or she was not rich and well dressed, was expected to make do with a poor, overpriced selection of merchandise, perhaps only two styles of boots or shoes and a few kinds of tableware, sold by truculent attendants in a laborious transaction that could not be guaranteed to result in acquisition of the wanted goods.

Modern Shopping

Thanks to the arrival of department stores, today shopping means freedom to look around, pick up objects, and ask questions—with no obligation whatsoever to buy. Department stores are known for promoting this sort of behavior. From the start, their architecture has, as one historian remarked, "encouraged a perception of the building as a public place, where consumption itself was almost incidental to the delights of a sheltered promenade in a densely crowded, middle-class urban space."[6] A department store is a destination where a person may enjoy pleasant surroundings and the sociability of the crowd while admiring beautiful things. Although they are private spaces, consumers have come to regard department stores as their temporary habitat, much as they would a park or a street corner.

Modern store managers were determined to create "walk-around" stores. Selfridge felt it was cheaper overall to let people circulate through the store than to police everyone who entered.[7] German stores were quick to institute a walk-around policy, which was appreciated by customers wishing to escape from the "crusty customs" of small shops where looking was discouraged.[8] At the Wertheim stores in Berlin around the turn of the last century, clerks were strictly instructed not to pressure shoppers to buy.

Modeling their store upon Marshall Field's and Wanamaker's, Tokyo's Mitsukoshi store readily adopted the policy of welcoming shoppers whether they bought or not. Earning a worldwide reputation for hospitality and politeness, the Japanese stores exceeded their American predecessors by placing greeters throughout the building.[9] At the opposite end of the spectrum was

BELOW LEFT Furniture department in the Grands Magasins du Louvre, early 20th century.

BELOW RIGHT Millinery department at Harrods, early 20th century.

BOTTOM Shoppers stroll through the Rudolph Hertzog fashion and fabrics specialty store in Berlin.

OPPOSITE A customer trying on a hat in the millinery department of a Karstadt store, ca. 1970.

FAR LEFT Photograph of shoppers on the stretch of Sixth Avenue known as New York City's "Ladies Mile," showing the elevated train on the left and the Siegel-Cooper store in the right foreground.

LEFT Attendants handle orders at the service desk, GUM, in Moscow ca. 1950. Browsing was not an option in this store.

Moscow's GUM, where no browsing was possible. Shoppers lined up at a counter and asked to see a particular item, which the clerk brought out for them to inspect. With demand high and supply limited, GUM clerks had power over customers, which often translated into bad behavior such as ignoring them, verbally abusing them, and refusing them merchandise.[10]

The department store was generally regarded as a women's paradise, as reflected in the title of Émile Zola's 1883 novel *Au Bonheur des dames*. A full 90 percent of the shoppers at Paris department stores in the 1880s were said to be women.[11] The effect of having free roaming rights in a store allowed them to believe that "the store is theirs, and that with propriety they may use it as they want to." Many women became shopping addicts, visiting department stores on an almost daily basis.[12] As Paris was under siege from the Prussian army in 1870, the Bon Marché and the Grands Magasins du Louvre closed because so many of their staff, then mainly men, had gone to the army. The public outcry at their closing was so great that they hired women clerks and reopened. Even as the Prussians encircled Paris and set explosives under bridges outside the city, American and English tourists continued to shop because for them leaving Paris without shopping in the major stores would "occasion life-long regret."[13]

World's fairs not only provided a model of how to display goods but also brought thousands of shoppers to the cities that held them. There was a synergy involved that the department stores counted on; they coordinated their featured merchandise and sales with displays and events at the exposition. Women tourists might claim that their destinations in Paris were museums and cathedrals, but shopping was "their paramount inspiration."[14] What woman had a "soul above dry goods?" wondered a fan of shopping who claimed to have witnessed a group of intellectual women living in her Paris boarding house who "day after day, throw books and papers aside and divide their time and thought between . . . two great dry goods centers."[15]

In New York, the shopping district known as "Ladies Mile" stretched along Broadway and Sixth Avenue between Fourteenth and Twenty-third streets in the 1890s.[16] The stores had transformed the old-fashioned, men-only city, focused on manufacturing and wholesaling and once characterized by filth and vice, into "female playgrounds" where respectable women could promenade with impunity.[17] Women visitors to New York skipped right past other attractions and headed straight to Ladies Mile when they came to town. A police station in the district got so many requests for directions that it posted a wall-sized tourist map with big red squares representing the department stores.[18]

Stirring the Crowds

Because department stores make profits from high volume and rapid turnover, they need to attract big crowds. Not only were crowds critical in furnishing buyers, but they were also part of the department store's displays, its decor, and its drama. A department store was absolutely dependent upon the enthusiasm, noise, and movement of masses of humanity.

Indeed, early department-store shopping was characterized by the "buzz of voices, the tramping of feet, the rapid gyrations of countless employés." By the 1860s it was said of Paris stores, "Go when you will, there is a surging crowd to jostle you at every step, and the manner in which you are carried along and tossed about recalls the billows of the sea."[19] The Bon Marché of the 1880s reportedly was visited daily by a "sea of humanity" of about 70,000 souls.[20] Holidays meant even larger crowds, up to 200,000 at Marshall Field in the early twentieth century.[21] During World War II, when American stores were mobbed, one store—unidentified, but almost certainly Macy's—was visited by a million people a day. The average number for large American stores was about 100,000 a day.[22] On the other hand, there was nothing more dismal than a massive, empty department store such as the former A. T. Stewart store in the 1890s before Wanamaker took it over. Being there was like strolling through a deserted palace where, a *New York Times* story reported, "only rare and disconsolate shopmen met the view."[23] The analogy often used for the apparent frenzy of activity witnessed in department stores was the hive. Mark Twain called the Louvre "a monster hive," Holland's de Bijenkorf stores are named for a beehive, and many American stores adopted Bee Hive as their nickname.[24] It took a while for some shoppers to adjust to the crowds. Some were overwhelmed by the masses surging in and out of the doors, clerks rushing around, and three-deep rows of shoppers fighting over goods piled onto bargain tables.[25] Parisian women of means, accustomed to patronizing couturiers, rejected department stores because they found the crowding vulgar. They soon adjusted, however. According to a British dry goods trade journal of 1874, "A few years ago, the crowding in these places was considered a drawback; the fear of vulgarity kept many away, but now it has become the fashion to patronise them, and it is considered quite the thing to be seen wandering through the galleries."[26] By the 1940s crowding had become an attraction rather than a detriment. Research showed that shoppers entering a store instinctively headed toward the brightest lights and loudest noise levels.[27] At Harrods' sales in January and July, shoppers regularly lined up outside the door hours before opening to be ready to claim bargains. A 1981 newspaper headline celebrated the joie de vivre expressed by shoppers with the headline "Dash it, Decorum Dies at Harrods."[28]

RIGHT A holiday crowd in front of the Myer Emporium, Melbourne, ca. 1930.

INSET Poster stamp showing modish young woman in front of Magasin du Nord, Copenhagen, ca. 1915.

FAR RIGHT Crowds jam the aisles of Helsinki's Stockmann department store during a 1950s "Ici Paris" promotion.

Japan's department stores have probably drawn larger crowds on a regular basis than any other stores in the world. Although it had not attained nearly the size it would after World War II, Mitsukoshi's new post-earthquake store of 1923 became so busy that it had to abandon traditional tatami mats for hardwood flooring. Shoppers were no longer required to exchange their street shoes for sandals as before. The effect of the change was to democratize shopping and further expand the number of shoppers, as people whose shoes were soiled and worn no longer had to suffer the humiliation of exposure when checking them at the door.[29] Sunday has long been the most popular day for Japanese department stores, which are filled not only with merchandise but with movie theaters, skating rinks, art galleries, and beer gardens.[30]

Department stores learned early to attract mobs of shoppers by putting on spectacles of all kinds, including special presentations of new merchandise called openings. Before World War I, openings usually took place three times a year: Spring, Fall, and Christmas. As the seasons changed, customers could expect to see glorious assemblages of the latest fashions in clothing and accessories, while at Christmastime stores were crammed with toys not seen during the rest of the year, particularly expensive dolls, mechanical toys, and wheeled vehicles.[31]

The era of grand openings was one of pomp and ceremony. The spring opening signaled the beginning of the Easter trade and started in March, about three weeks before the holiday. To mark the occasion, stores hired orchestras and festooned their interiors with lavish decorations, typically consisting of real or artificial flowers in huge vases or trailing around pillars and across ceilings, tall "trees," and up to a thousand caged live birds.[32] After the opening, shoppers could expect to get good buys on canaries.[33]

Christmas

By the mid-twentieth century, however, openings had become less important. Although there were still spring and fall collections, change in the fashion world was taking place so rapidly that new styles were introduced into stores year round. Toys were no longer bought only at Christmas; indeed, by the 1920s most stores had permanent toy departments. But these changes did not diminish the importance of Christmas as an occasion for special events. In fact, Christmas was celebrated more than ever before in the 1920s, with parades, Santa Clauses, walk-through Christmas villages and grottoes, mammoth fir trees, Christmas carols sung by employee choral groups, clever mechanical window displays, and elaborate lighted decorations adorning exterior facades and interiors.[34] In the English-speaking countries, department stores knew no limit in devising Christmas festivities,

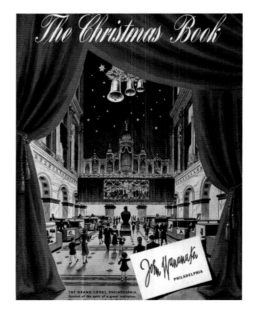

especially those aimed at children. Throughout England, Australia, and the United States, Santa Claus and Father Christmas figures had appeared in dry goods, variety, and department stores as far back as the 1870s, perhaps even earlier. Although scarcely a department store when it was founded in New York City, Macy's nonetheless established itself as headquarters for Santa from its first year, 1858. If this is indeed accurate, as the store claimed in an advertisement in 1902, it would make Macy's the first retailer to have installed a Santa Claus on its premises. By the 1890s Santa was well established in many department stores, where he was enthroned in a grotto or fairyland, dispensing balloons and trinkets to children. In the 1920s many North American stores added Santa Claus parades and other holiday events to their annual calendars. Santa would often arrive at a department store at the endpoint of just such a parade to kick off the opening of the store's toyland. Keeping up with the times, he traveled by the latest means of transportation, sometimes landing on store roofs in a dirigible or helicopter.

Santa's visits grew ever more elaborate in the 1920s and 1930s, and the jolly man's seasonal reign was extended to include photo sessions, parties, and breakfasts and lunches with children. In the 1930s London's Marshall & Snelgrove hosted Christmas teas for children, with entertainers and a gift for each from the tree.[35] Many stores created their own "brand-name" sidekicks to Santa, such as Uncle Mistletoe, Christmas Carol, and Mr. Bingle. Holiday entertainment has included clowns performing magic tricks, circuses with wild animals, and carnival rides on store roofs. Walk-through Christmas villages, particularly those with buildings and characters fabricated by the Christian Hofmann Company in Germany, were enormously popular in the United States.

European countries have flirted with Santa, whether he was known as Père Noël, der Weihnachtsmann, or by other names, but, partly because of the popularity of outdoor Christmas markets, he's never become as deeply lodged in store traditions on the Continent. When he does appear, he rarely holds court, but wanders around departments or on the sidewalk outside giving away small favors. On the other hand, gaily decorated trees and exterior scenes and decorations created by twinkling lights have long been popular, and extensive window displays showing miniature snow-clad Christmas villages or children around the tree receiving gifts have drawn crowds of families for decades. Huge decorated Christmas trees have always been a favorite in stores designed with lofty rotundas, such as Galeries Lafayette in Paris, Sterling-Lindner in Cleveland, and The Emporium in San Francisco. At Marshall Field's, the huge tree arising from the center of the Walnut Room was decorated by workers suspended on wires and required a staff of firefighters on guard round the clock.[36]

Poster advertising the Christmas toy department at de Bijenkorf in Amsterdam, mid-1950s.

Santa greets children at John Wanamaker, Philadelphia, 1926.

OPPOSITE A child reaches for a doll at a Karstadt department store, 1970s.

De Bijenkorf, Amsterdam, 1913. The Colonialist caricature of an unclothed, dark-skinned figure surrounded by white goods presumed the superiority of European consumers with spotless linens.

Special Sales

Like Christmas, special sales also provided a reason to introduce ballyhoo and hoopla into department stores. Sales and fairs, with their loads of merchandise stacked and piled, raised on plinths, and draped over stands, enlivened mundane shopping and turned it into a show. The "occasion," a sale for which every effort was made to create a sense of something special taking place, was a concept closely related to openings. Between the two, occasions and openings, stores began to develop an annual calendar of events for which certain merchandise was amassed, spotlighted, and made the centerpiece in a festival lasting days or weeks. A successfully arranged calendar had the advantage of attracting crowds and evening out the peaks and valleys of selling by scheduling merchandising attractions during predictably slack times.

As was true of so many of department stores' marketing innovations, Aristide Boucicaut was the first to come up with the idea of a special sale that would focus on white goods. According to legend, he was inspired by a heavy blanket of snow that brought Paris to a halt and from this built the "blanc" into the store's "single most important sales week of the year."[37] His idea, which involved wrapping the interior in white cloth, was soon borrowed by other Paris department stores, as well as stores in other countries. Although almost all American stores and some in England adopted the idea of the white sale, even sending employees to Paris to learn how it was done, few took on the significance of white sales in Paris, for which all of France became involved in producing, selling, and buying linens and associated goods. Women all over the country were said to study the catalogs. Goods sold in the sales, held in late January or early February, were unique, made exclusively for these occasions and available only then. Each store had its own sources, often whole villages of women sewing at home.[38]

In Germany, the department-store chain of Hermann Tietz rivaled France in its enthusiasm for week-long white sales known as *Weisse Woche*. The windows and interior were transformed into all-white spectacles of bed linens, handkerchiefs, underwear, white clothing, and cotton, linen, and silk sold by the piece and by the yard. Other departments also displayed white merchandise such as porcelain, enamel ware, shoes, scarves, umbrellas, giftware, jewelry, even groceries. Other German department stores followed suit, but none could match the Tietz stores. The store commissioned merchandise from manufacturers a year in advance to get unique goods at special prices. White sales were so popular with the German public that, even though small shopkeepers hated them, they were expressly exempted from laws enacted by the Nazis forbidding special department-store sales.[39]

A standard calendar of annual sales and expositions began to jell in the 1880s and 1890s.[40] The year typically began with a white sale, moved on through special promotions of curtains, spring clothing clearances, straw hats, and summer sales. Before the advent of air conditioning, business fell off during the summer, so stores sometimes laid off workers and tried to get rid of lingering merchandise then. September brought displays of furniture and Oriental carpets, and in October and November winter clothing was featured. Small items such as ornamental boxes, combs, and fans, many of them handmade in Paris, where they were known as *articles de Paris*, were abundant in December and meant for Christmas and New Year's gifts.[41] Another occasion to fit into the calendar was the store's anniversary. American stores made much of the anniversaries of their founding, real or invented. Old customers were invited to bring in items bought by their elder relatives for display at this time, an ever-popular custom. More than one observer has noticed how often a store anniversary "never exactly marks the true anniversary date, but falls in a month which seems convenient for the store."[42]

Some stores presented merchandise fairs during slow months. Stanley Marcus openly admitted that Neiman Marcus's "Fortnights," borrowed from Stockholm's Nordiska department store, were intended "to help us overcome a historical business lag, which always occurred in mid-October." At a time when other stores often ran anniversary sales, his store brought in "large quantities of fine merchandise" and "turned October into a month of peak traffic, even surpassing Christmas." Fortnights became a longstanding tradition in the Dallas store.[43]

Special sales conducted with major publicity campaigns and associated events differed sharply from the chronic sales held by bargain emporiums. Although almost all department stores had bargain days, usually Friday, too-frequent sales held for no good reason were seen as the mark of a cheap and disreputable store, and may account for why Wanamaker held only one sale a year in its first years, dubbed "annual lowering day."[44] Early department stores in Germany were criticized for spurious sales that lasted only briefly or offered severely limited quantities.[45] In the late nineteenth and early twentieth centuries some American stores held "one-hour" sales with "drastic reductions," often accompanied by bugles or trumpets. In 1899 an unscrupulous store in Chicago was known for sales at which dollar items were reduced to ninety-eight cents, while "twenty-five cent articles would be offered at a bargain for *forty cents* 'today only.'"[46] Department stores interested in attracting more affluent customers eliminated these practices by the 1920s.[47]

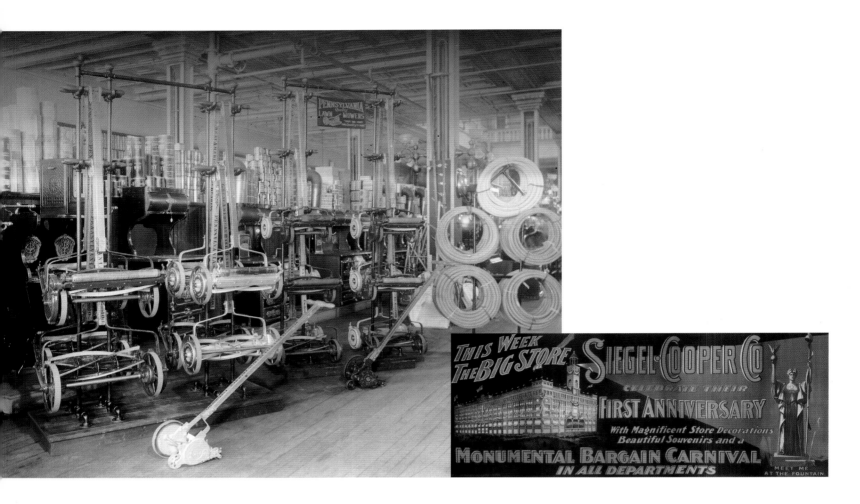

Worlds of Goods

Dry goods stores and other small specialty shops began to expand into large emporiums offering goods of all kinds as a means of cushioning the economic unpredictability involved in selling only one kind of merchandise. Having modeled his store on the Crystal Palace exhibition of 1851, by the 1890s William Whiteley had realized his dream of replicating the fair by assembling a great variety of things from all over the world under one roof. It could be said of his store and others like it that the wealth of goods, as well as the grand buildings, marble staircases, and "the great concourse of people" seemed "to arouse . . . feelings of pleasure and satisfaction second only to those experienced on a visit to a world's fair."[48]

A few stores, such as Selfridges in London and The Emporium in San Francisco, began as full-blown department stores, but the majority grew from retail shops and wholesaling businesses. Most often they developed out of the dry goods trade, which, in the later nineteenth century, was primarily involved with textiles. Stores coming from this tradition included the Bon Marché, Mitsukoshi, and Wertheim's. Other origins included men's and boys clothing (Wanamaker's); fancy goods (Macy's); tea (Harrods); furniture (Frederick & Nelson); dry goods wholesaling (Stewart's, Marshall Field); furs (Halle's, Hudson Bay Company); and general stores (ZCMI, David Jones). Many had only a handful of departments when they started. Fifteen was about average in the mid-1880s, an unimpressive number compared to the 100–125 departments typically found in big stores by 1910.[49]

Other stores, such as The Fair in Chicago, Bernheimer's in Baltimore, and many German stores of the 1890s, began as bargain bazaars specializing in household goods and having no fixed merchandise lines. Historians have speculated that the bargain store represents a far more common type of early department store than does the upscale "marble palace" celebrated for its carriage-trade customers.[50] Bargain department stores were typically stocked with whatever was currently being sacrificed in the marketplace. This kind of merchandising was so common in the early decades of American department-store growth that bankrupt stocks and closeouts were routinely depleted, creating an opportunity for the growth of "bargain-making industries" that produced cheap and imitation goods for department stores. American-made "Oriental" rugs were a prime example—proponents even asked for special tariffs to protect this "native industry" from overseas competition, notably from Germany.[51] In Germany, anti-department-store critics referred to merchandise sold in the large emporiums at the turn of the century as junk—*Ramsch-Artikel* or *Talmi-Eleganz*—while in France the terms *faux-luxe* and *pacotille* were used to describe the showy,

CANDIES FOR THE HOLIDAY SEASON

THE FINEST OF CHOCOLATES, PUT UP IN VERY HANDSOME CONTAINERS. THEY ARE PARTICULARLY SUITABLE FOR EITHER CHILDREN OR ADULTS, BEING MOST ATTRACTIVE AS STOCKING FILLERS, CHRISTMAS TREE DECORATIONS, OR FOR CHURCH ENTERTAINMENTS.

HANDSOMELY DECORATED DAINTY APPEARANCE

V3-827. Useful Sugar Sifter, ruby glass, nickel-plated top, containing chocolates. Each.... **25c**

V3-828. Jap China Cup and Saucer, packed with chocolates. Each.... **15c**

V3-829. China Mug, decorated with juvenile figures, packed with chocolates. Each.......... **15c**

V3-830. Mechanical Toy Automobile, fitted with strong spring, heavily loaded with chocolates, a very superior article. Each **75c**

V3-831. China Dog and Basket, packed with chocolates. Each.. **15c**

V3-832. Fancy China Teapot, marine decoration, useful size, packed with chocolates. Each **50c**

V3-833. Handsome Toy Row Boat, with oars, well modelled, packed with chocolates. Boy's favorite. Each................... **45c**

V3-834. Dainty China Tea Set, beautiful floral decoration, filled with high-grade chocolates. A very serviceable gift. Per set.................... **1.50** Extra Cups and Saucers, each.............. **25c**

V3-835. Glass Sugar Shaker, filled with chocolates. Ea. **15c**

V3-836. China Boy and Basket, packed with chocolates. Each **25c** See also V3-806.

V3-837. China Butter Dish, very dainty, and of a serviceable size, packed with chocolates. Each....... **25c**

V3-838. Neat Straw Basket, filled with high-grade chocolates. Each **25c**

V3-845. Dainty Cup and Saucer, packed with chocolates. Each....... **25c**

V3-839. Leatherette Hand-bag, packed with chocolates, girls' favorite. Each.... **25c**

V3-840. Toy Telephone, packed with chocolates. Each.... **25c**

ORDER EARLY

V3-841. Novelty Owl Cream Jug, packed with very fine chocolates, useful article. Ea. **25c**

V3-842. Dainty China Cream Jug and Basin, packed with chocolates. Each..... **25c**

V3-843. Set of Three Novelties, packed with chocolates, sold only in sets. Per set........................ **25c**

V3-844. Set of Three China Novelties, packed with chocolates, sold only in sets. Per set **25c**

V3-846. China Dog, loaded with chocolates. Each. **25c**

V3-847. Glass Bowl, antique style, daintily tinted, a very serviceable gift, packed with chocolates. Each.......... **50c**

V3-848. China Tan Boot, filled with chocolates. Each.......... **15c**

V3-849. Mechanical Walking Man and Barrow, loaded with chocolates. Each. .. **25c**

V3-850. Handsome Straw Basket, filled with choice chocolates of assorted flavors. Each.......... **60c**

V3-851. Handsomely Lacquered Handkerchief Box, packed with chocolates, a very acceptable gift. Each **50c**

OPPOSITE Eaton's 1913 holiday gift catalog featuring chocolate candies in attractive and unusual containers.

BELOW LEFT Neckpieces of beaded jet meant to be sewn onto dresses, Bon Marché catalog, ca. 1900.

BELOW RIGHT Holiday giftware department at de Bijenkorf, The Hague.

mass-produced goods sold in department stores, as opposed to those of fine design and materials made by traditional artisans.[52] By the 1920s, however, many department stores that had begun as bargain bazaars had evolved into purveyors of middle-class goods.

The Bon Marché began to expand from piece goods to ladies' coats and cloaks before 1860 and by 1869 the store had adopted the departmental system of organization, in which each department had its own manager who selected the merchandise and ran it as though it were a small shop.[53] Whiteley began with fabrics and in the late 1860s added gloves, jewelry, furs, umbrellas, and artificial flowers.[54] By the mid-1870s the stock of an English draper's shop included "china ornaments, gilded nicknacks of all kinds, work-baskets, albums, every sort of thing in Japan ware and Morocco leather, purses, [and] pocketbooks" as well as the usual handkerchiefs and "cartloads of cravats." At Christmas the sorts of things customarily given as gifts—toys, bibelots, and bonbon boxes—would be added to the assortment, both in Paris and London stores, to attract customers who ordinarily would have gone elsewhere for these things.[55]

Every expansion in merchandise upset traditionalists who believed specialization was the hallmark of a quality shop. "Whither are we drifting?" asked the *Warehousemen and Drapers' Trade Journal*, an English publication that monitored retailing developments in Britain and France. From the journal's point of view it was bad enough that dry goods establishments handled soap and traveling bags, but would it end there? No, there were also valentines and shoes and "imitation jet" jewelry. Soon, the editor mused, it would be common "for an assistant to be asked for a pound of blue paint, six-penny worth of tenpenny nails, the latest novel, or a glass of 'mother in law,'" the last a digestive concoction.[56] Exactly when these wares arrived in English stores is uncertain, but all could certainly be purchased at Chicago's department store The Fair a few decades later.[57]

Whiteleys handled very diverse lines of merchandise. When Charles Dickens' son wrote about the store, imagining himself as a customer whose needs were taken care of by the Universal Provider from babyhood to old age, he was struck by one of the Provider's newest departments, which supplied "the beef and mutton, the tea and coffee, the poultry and game, of everyday life" as well as other foodstuffs. To provision this department Whiteley had recently bought a farm.[58] There seemed to be nothing the store didn't deal in, including artificial limbs, cooking ranges, ferrets, guns, poultry, steam engines, surgical instruments, and yachting supplies.[59]

The *Warehousemen and Drapers' Trade Journal* was not alone in its concerns over the rapaciousness of department stores. Under the title "Dry Goods and Fish," an American newspaper edi-

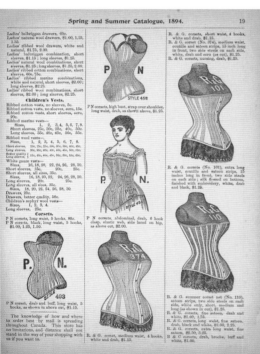

torial commented, "It is hard to see where these department stores will stop." The statement was precipitated by a large department store in Chicago, probably The Fair, which had contracted with a big fishery on Lake Michigan to supply its entire catch—up to 25,000 pounds—to the store each week. The store planned to sell fish that usually went for nine cents a pound for only four cents.[60]

Far from bargains in fish, Paris stores, along with more upscale "carriage trade" stores in other countries, tended to specialize more in fabrics and fashion goods and less in household items. Most other stores that would become great department stores, such as Altman's, Marshall Field, and the Grands Magasins du Louvre, dealt primarily in dry goods and certain items of women's attire in the mid-1880s. However, by the start of the twentieth century it was commonplace to carry diversified merchandise and only a few large stores still focused solely on their stock of respectable dry goods. The "better" stores continued to custom-produce women's clothing to a limited degree, but more and more apparel was being produced outside store salons, and factory-made women's clothing was about to become widely available.

Expansion into a wide variety of merchandise to cushion seasonal and price fluctuations in specific lines did not come easily for some stores, which feared their reputations would be harmed. Department stores specializing in dry goods and custom-made apparel considered themselves above the level of the universal provider stores precisely because they did *not* handle every sort of merchandise. As John Wanamaker would later say of his store in a speech to the American Academy of Political and Social Science, "This store of today was not and never will be of the class known as 'department store.' It does not deal in liquors, groceries, drugs or 'everything that can be sold at a profit.'"[61] In 1887 Marshall Field restricted its four selling floors to dry goods, hosiery, muslin underwear, suits, cloaks, shawls, carpets, upholstery, and furs. Field specifically resisted book selling, which he considered low class because of how poorly books were typically handled by large dry goods retailers.[62]

In every country there were two kinds of department stores: the *Kaufhaus* and *Warenhaus* in Germany; the *grand magasin* and *bazar* in France. Wanamaker couldn't bear to call his store a department store, for many years referring to it simply as "a new kind of store." Marshall Field chose to call its departments "sections" instead. In Canada, Eaton's preferred to call itself a "departmental" store, as though the addition of "al" could distinguish it from the bargain bazaar.

Expanding into new merchandise lines courted peril for a store that wanted to hold itself aloof from the common herd. Eaton's competitor Simpson's gingerly expanded its offerings by adding boots and shoes to its dry goods base, then installing a tea counter, and so on. But Simpson's proprietor admitted he was being cautious because he didn't want "to have a store which people would enter or leave by stealth, and of whose trademark the public would be in any sense ashamed."[63] Simpson's concerns were not imaginary. In Germany, the upper middle class of the 1890s and early 1900s did not want to be seen in a *Warenhaus*. To save face, they might say they were shopping on behalf of their servants or ask that their purchases be wrapped in plain paper.[64]

Certain types of merchandise were particularly controversial, notably meat, liquor, and books. All three were strenuously opposed by small storekeepers who felt threatened by the large stores' ability to undersell them, yet each was challenged on distinctly different grounds. The issue with some goods was the question of *who* was allowed to consume them. Because the department store, unlike a neighborhood store, was large and impersonal, anyone could buy anything without questions being asked or rumors spreading. Liquor was an issue in the United States, where the temperance movement, widely embraced by middle-class women, had stigmatized consumption of spirits, particularly by the gentler sex. In a similar vein, there was some concern about how easily women could obtain silk underwear and cosmetics. Many stores avoided displaying underwear in their windows, and Selfridges sold rouge and lipstick under the counter before World War I.[65]

Meat raised very different issues. Department-store opponents tried to create a furor, mostly unsuccessfully, about the "seemliness" of selling certain goods alongside others that were considered strikingly dissimilar. In Germany the charge was made that the Jewish *Grossbazare*, as the nineteenth-century department store was insultingly called, was as lowly as the Oriental bazaar—which was presumed to be a crude and primitive type of commerce in which anything could be sold indiscriminately.[66] In Chicago opponents managed to get an ordinance passed that prohibited selling meat in department stores, but a judge ruled it illegitimate. The issue gradually waned in the United States, yet, judging by a *New Yorker* piece in 1928, negative attitudes about mixed merchandise tended to persist. In a light feature story about Bloomingdale's basement, the author conveyed an amused hauteur, saying, "No where else that we know of can one run such an exciting gamut of sandwiches, poinsettias, cushion treads, dressed veal, step-ins, Haviland china, postcards for Mother's birthday, and Almond Krunch."[67]

Food selling in department stores came under attack once again when the Nazis came to power in Germany. The presence of a grocery department became a criterion that characterized the objectionable *Warenhaus*. In September 1933 the Ministry of Economics declared that a *Warenhaus* was officially defined as "a marketing outlet . . . in which goods of many types that

ABOVE The supermarket in Nordiska Kompaniet in Stockholm, ca. 1950.

do not belong together, including groceries, are offered for sale." Although KaDeWe's grocery department was a popular feature with shoppers from the time the store opened in 1907, its right to exist in the store had never been accepted by the small tradesmen who supported the Nazis.[68] Considering the early agitation over department stores selling meat, it is interesting how much the status of these comestibles changed over time, particularly in Harrods, KaDeWe, and many Japanese stores. Harrods' meat, fish, and game displays, not to mention the vast variety of cheeses, butter, and other food items, are legendary.[69] In KaDeWe, shoppers can count on having a thousand types of sausages to choose from and have been able to buy puma steak and lion meat, along with cheeses and other food items from all over the world.[70] The difference, obviously, between contemporary food departments and those found in the past is that the modern emporia are often stocked with delicacies meant to delight gourmet consumers with their rarity and fine quality, whereas in the early days stores mainly provided staple foodstuffs of no special gastronomic distinction. At the same time, ordinary consumers of the early twentieth century often felt that department-store grocery departments enabled them to buy foodstuffs that had once been luxuries to them, such as the oranges, tomatoes, and canned vegetables sold at reduced prices by Tietz in Munich. The flavor of tomatoes was completely unknown to most Germans when Tietz introduced them in 1908 and was at first a shock to the public.[71]

A different kind of controversy attached to the sale of books. Some felt that selling them in department stores devalued and degraded them. Independent booksellers, who feared they would be wiped out by the big stores' specially printed lower-priced editions, portrayed the bargain books as poorly produced and of no literary value.[72] German critics insinuated that the big stores might as well sell books and sheet music by weight, which they parodied as, "I'll take a quarter pound of Mozart, please."[73] Wertheim's own publishing house, the Globus Verlag, employed a stable of authors who churned out popular novels and works on sport, gardening, and cooking.[74] Although publishers joined with booksellers in protest, the fact was that often the plates used by the department stores to print bargain volumes came from publishing houses that resold them when demand had been exhausted for the full-priced editions.[75] Salman Schocken, who would one day establish Schocken Books and publish Franz Kafka and Martin Buber, reflected a radically different point of view. He felt that his book department furnished the working class with the kind of reading material routinely enjoyed by the middle class.[76]

Sooner or later, most of the once-dubious merchandise was accepted as legitimate, though there were a few stores such as Wanamaker's that avoided liquor. Most eventually dealt in gro-

ceries, meat, silk underwear, cosmetics, and books. A book department, in fact, eventually came to be seen as adding prestige to a store. Department stores began to boast of the completeness of their merchandise lines. No longer a tea shop, by the 1890s Harrods had adopted a slogan appropriate to the British Empire, *Omnia Omnibus Ubique*, which went Whiteleys one better, adding to his implicit "Everything for Everybody" the extension "Everywhere."[77] In deciding what merchandise to carry, department stores were more than eager to follow popular trends. During the bicycle craze of the late 1890s they sold bicycles by the thousands, followed by pianos, the modern family's entertainment center of that era.[78] In Japan the spread of merchandise also moved forward. Venerable dry goods and kimono firms that traced their ancestry back to the 1600s confronted competition from hypermarkets located in commuter train stations. By the 1930s the two types began to converge, as the veteran department stores, which had been fashion oriented, began carrying daily necessities, while the station stores went upscale with fashion merchandise.[79]

Merchandise handled by a full-fledged department store ran the gamut from the excessively mundane to the exotic, with no shortage of the former. Knit underwear, for example, was core merchandise. Stores in cold climates, such as Eaton's in Toronto and other Canadian cities, stocked a goodly measure of woolen undershirts.[80] The Mormon department store ZCMI produced overalls and underwear under its own label.[81] Salman Schocken used his clout as a merchant to influence men's underwear choices in Germany, encouraging them to abandon woolen underwear for more "healthful" boxer shorts.[82]

Big stores depended upon other staples too. Meeting customer need was something of a mission among department stores and sometimes led to unusual departments. If a store received many requests for a certain item, it had to accommodate the demand. During World War I Halle's opened a Military Shop so that families could remedy the government's slowness in outfitting soldiers.[83] It was probably the same logic that led Filene's in Boston and Bernheimer's in Baltimore to install dairies complete with cows and milking equipment in their stores during the era when milk supplies were often adulterated.[84]

Unusual merchandise abounds in the long history of department stores, including enough live animals to fill many zoos. In 1896 a cartoon in *Puck* showed an imaginary department store of the near future with a sign that announced "Bargain Sale at the Wild Animal Counter To-Day."[85] The notion wasn't so fantastic. In the 1880s Whiteleys had a "zoological department." Whiteley liked to boast of how quickly he could obtain a white elephant on order.[86] In the 1890s the Siegel-

TOP Cosmetics and perfumes at Harrods, ca. 1920.

ABOVE Fine jewelry and objets d'art at Harrods, ca. 1900.

Cooper stores had a large pet department in which it sold the usual domestic pets, as well as monkeys and lion and panther cubs.[87] Bernheimer's surprised Baltimore with a startling advertisement for "Live Horses" amid its notices for carpets and women's dresses in the 1920s, but explained that they had been acquired from a government auction and were appropriate for its customer base, which included farmers and teamsters.[88] Although most stores limited pet departments to canaries, sales of wildlife did not end in the early decades of department stores. At least one Tokyo store auctioned racehorses in the 1970s, and it became a summertime tradition to gather crickets from the countryside and place them in enclosed store gardens to the delight of children who were permitted to "hunt" them for their collections.[89]

Like the forerunner dry goods stores, department stores carried luxury merchandise alongside commonplace necessities. After all, a basic organizing principle of department stores was that shoppers came to the store for necessities and left with little indulgences that filled unrecognized needs. In the 1880s critics said that the Paris stores put out bait to lure women inside, "inciting their customers to luxury and extravagance."[90] Customers at A. T. Stewart's store in the 1850s commented that Stewart sold "sixpenny calicos" as well as fabulously expensive cobweb laces.[91] The store was celebrated for merchandise such as lace handkerchiefs priced at $150 and "bride's boxes" consisting of lace veiling, flounces, and trimmings that started at $1,500, a truly princess-ly sum in the 1850s. It was also known for magnificent shawls that Stewart's agents were said to have purchased from aristocratic women of Europe for sums up to $5,000.[92] Marshall Field expanded its luxury merchandise in anticipation of the 1893 World's Columbian Exposition, buying Paris couture, $20,000 Persian rugs, Chinese jades, and antique furniture. After the fair, the store continued to send buyers abroad to bring back laces from Brussels and Calais, silks from Lyons, and sables from Russia.[93]

It seems necessary, however, to point out that luxury goods always formed a relatively small part of the overall merchandise mix. As an economist would observe in 1919, the department store "cannot as a rule build a large enough trade on exclusive lines to make the business pay."[94] Relatively few stores—and only those in large cities with millions of visitors—can attract enough wealthy customers to specialize in luxury goods. Yet almost all department stores have historically offered a sampling of prestige merchandise to lend their stores a reputation for style and to create a sense of what's been called "exclusiveness for the masses."[95] The owners of Berlin's first Wertheim store, for instance, grasped in the 1890s that its "outstanding success was due to its presenting an astute mix of mass products and luxury articles."[96] In a 1926–1927 an-

LEFT Carpet display at Printemps in Paris, ca. 1930.

niversary publication Lord & Taylor acknowledged that the project of the modern store was to "redeem the monotony of mass production by adopting ideas from twenty centuries of art."[97] The same is true of Bloomingdale's, which succeeded in earning a reputation for stylishness by including a "small increment of merchandise that is trend-setting" among the basics. This merchandise built a "psychological showcase for the everyday stuff."[98]

Inexpensive luxuries sold in nineteenth-century department stores included *articles de Paris*. These small objects, handcrafted by Parisian artisans in home workshops, were offered not only in Paris stores but in London and America as well. They were particularly popular as Christmas and New Year's gifts. Artificial flowers may have been the quintessential *article de Paris*, but there were many other things too, such as decorative bonbon boxes that could later be used for gloves or handkerchiefs, as well as buttons of horn or papier-mâché, parasols, fans, and dolls.[99] For a time the rage was for objects that resembled something else, such as brass inkwells that looked like miniature umbrella stands or bells for the dining room that reproduced a dining table realistically set for a meal with a pyramided plate of ice cream in the middle hiding the spring.[100]

Handmade goods often shared display space with factory-made merchandise. The Bon Marché filled its show windows at Christmastime with exquisite needlework hand stitched by nuns, while Wertheim showed colorful appliquéd panels of monkeys, storks, and hens by Katy Münchhausen.[101] Buyers were always eager to acquire handcrafted goods for their stores, ranging from chenille bedspreads made in the American South at Marshall Field to beaded dresses bought by the gross for next to nothing in France by American stores immediately after World War I.[102]

Some department stores created styles and produced merchandise of their own. Before World War I Paris stores set up design studios for decorative housewares and furniture. The objects they produced were initially handcrafted but later made in limited editions in factories in and around Paris. In 1912 Printemps established Atelier Primavera to design and produce modern decorative objects. Beginning with ceramics, the atelier soon branched into glassware and bronzes as well as carpets, wallpapers, textiles, and furniture. By 1925 Primavera had a substantial staff of designers, draftsmen, and artisans, as well as connections with more than three hundred more artisans in Paris and beyond. In 1930 the products of Atelier Primavera were hailed as inexpensive objets d'art exceeding nine thousand original designs, the value of which certainly would—and did—grow over time. The Grands Magasins du Louvre embarked on a similar project called Studium Louvre in 1922, while the Bon Marché had its Atelier Pomone, and the Galeries Lafayette established La Maîtrise.[103] Beginning in the 1920s, the Magasins Réunis also sold original modern decorative art

— MAISON. A. BOUCICAUT — PARIS

DE L'ATELIER D'ART POMONE

GRANDS MAGASINS
DE LA
SAMARITAINE
PARIS

Largeur 80

PRIX 1f05

SINS
AINE

Largeur 80

PRIX 1f05

PRIMAVERA
ATELIER D'ART
DES MAGASINS DU
PRINTEMPS

CHAMBRE à COUCHER
de LOUIS SOGNOT

PAVILLON du PRINTEMPS EXPOSITION des ARTS DECORATIFS
PRIMAVERA MEUBLE
INSTALLE
DECORE

STIL

Våren sommaren
1 9 3 2
A.B. Nordiska Kompaniet

OPPOSITE Cover of Nordiska's style magazine, Stockholm, Summer 1932. Department stores were among the first retailers to promote the modern furniture styles of the 20th century.

LEFT Modern ceramics on display during a Scandinavian exposition at Stockmann in Helsinki, ca. 1950.

ABOVE Adam Gimbel, Frederic Gimbel, and Bernard Gimbel looking at Della Robbia's *Madonna and Child*, from the art collection of William Randolph Hearst, to be sold in the New York Gimbels store in a huge sale in 1941.

crafted by designers and artists in Nancy.[104] The studios of the four big stores were represented at the 1925 Exposition des Arts Décoratifs, each in its own luxuriant modern building, which housed opulent bedrooms and living rooms displaying furnishings produced by the studios. Sweden's N. K. became a leading manufacturer of furniture in the Scandinavian modern style in the 1940s and 1950s. Designer Astrid Sampe, head of the store's textile department for decades, revolutionized the country's styling of industrially made textiles.[105]

Certain types of luxury goods such as Oriental carpets and antique objects and furniture—and airplanes in the twentieth century—brought status to department stores. In the 1880s Paris stores, which did not deal in furniture to any extent until the 1890s, selected September for exhibits of carpets and antique fabrics, presenting customers with wares from Persia, India, Daghestan, and other Eastern regions. Some customers sneered at these exhibits, characterizing them as "the wreck of past centuries, the bric-à-brac of whole countries," an attitude that would emerge again when Lord & Taylor put a collection of "Romanov treasures" up for sale in 1933 (see image on page 250), and once more in 1941 when Gimbels and Saks (which Gimbels owned) liquidated part of the vast collection of William Randolph Hearst.[106] Although the Russian goods, which included priests' vestments, icons, and Fabergé jewelry, were billed as relics from royal palaces, an alternative viewpoint described them as "the debris of Russian hotels, monasteries, shops, and palaces."[107] The Hearst sale, managed by brothers Armand and Victor Hammer, involved fifteen thousand objects ranging from an entire monastery to armorial helmets and included a gold Benvenuto Cellini bowl with a jewel-encrusted base.[108] In the words of Victor Hammer, the plan was to "sell daggers for letter-openers, parts of armor for paperweights, and shields for foyers."[109] With a bit of imagination there was little that could not be sold to American customers looking for exotic relics of the past. Neiman Marcus collected South American molas, Kashmir shawls, and Bedouin robes to have them remade into decorative hostess gowns and tote bags.[110]

The imported goods carrying the greatest status were French, but many stores also relied upon England for prestige merchandise, particularly men's tailored clothes and furnishings. As early as the 1880s Shirokiya arranged with a British supplier to obtain clothing stock.[111] Moscow's Muir and Merrielees preferred British goods but regretfully was forced to import much of its merchandise from Germany at the time of the Russian Revolution.[112] American stores, as well as those in Canada and Australia, prized British woolens and sportswear in the 1920s, depending upon English and European "treasure houses" to meet the growing demand for stylish goods of premier quality not available in North America.[113] Wartime revealed how much the newer nations, such as the U.S.,

Canada, and Australia, relied upon the "old country" for goods as well as for style leadership.[114] Although they developed their own fashion industries in the twentieth century, they could not entirely break free of Europe and Britain. Eaton's noted in a 1944 advertisement that its stocks of British merchandise were running low, but that their buyers were ready to go abroad "as soon as civilian travel becomes officially permissible." It reassured its customers that it was looking forward to peacetime, when, "As of Yore Britain Will Deliver the Goods . . . and Eaton's Will Sell Them!"[115] Somewhat surprisingly, as it was a nation known more for industrial proficiency than for style, a number of department stores worldwide looked to the United States for imports. American goods may not have possessed high status but were attractive nonetheless for their utilitarian value, technical sophistication, and, increasingly, as symbols of a powerful nation's popular culture. Around 1907 the German department store Leonhard Tietz acquired much of its merchandise in the United States, including shoes, glassware, and house furnishings—even as U.S. stores bought notions, toys, and other merchandise from Germany.[116] About a decade later, British-run department stores in Singapore acquired shoes, underwear, and large appliances from American sources.[117] In addition to such mundane goods, stores in various countries imported American curiosities. How odd that Harrods advertised the grotesquely comic Billiken figurine, "the god of things as they ought to be," as a Christmas gift in 1908![118]

At the import fairs that were so popular in department stores worldwide in the 1960s and later, American stores featured the designs and products of Italy, Japan, China, France, and other nations, while those stores reciprocated with American fairs. La Rinascente presented pine furniture and pewter accessories from the United States to satisfy Italian consumer interest in Early American furniture, which was strong in the 1960s.[119] Galeries Lafayette promoted American merchandise under the rubric of the "Life of an American Woman" named Pat. As is so often true of cultural translations, slip-ups occurred now and then. A French woman at the exhibit was surprised when a journalist told her that downing a shot of bourbon at a snack bar, presented as an American custom, did not in fact figure prominently in the shopping ritual of most New York women.[120] No doubt Chinese women would have been equally chagrined to see underpants stamped "Bloomies" in English and Chinese characters for sale during Bloomingdale's 1980 Chinese festival.[121]

The wide variety in department-store offerings did not last. After the 1980s, holding on to their identities as universal providers would become a difficult task for most surviving department stores. Many found it necessary to eliminate departments that lost money, but it is surprising how long some stores continued to provide a broad range of merchandise. Hudson's, for instance, maintained its home furnishings departments long past the point that it was profitable.[122] Even as it extended its fashion emphasis, Eaton's stood committed to carrying all kinds of goods. As Fredrick Eaton commented in 1985, "You cannot retreat from any of these businesses in a department store."[123]

At import fairs, department stores featured merchandise from all around the world. Japanese style is celebrated in a Karstadt window during a Japanese festival, ca. 1980 (below left). A poster for a Chinese exhibition at de Bijenkorf in Holland, 1983 (below right). Asian festival at a Globus department store, Chur, Switzerland, in 1931 (opposite).

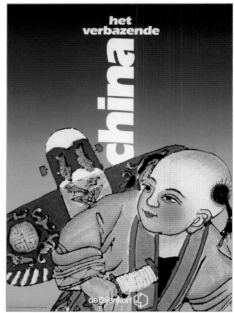

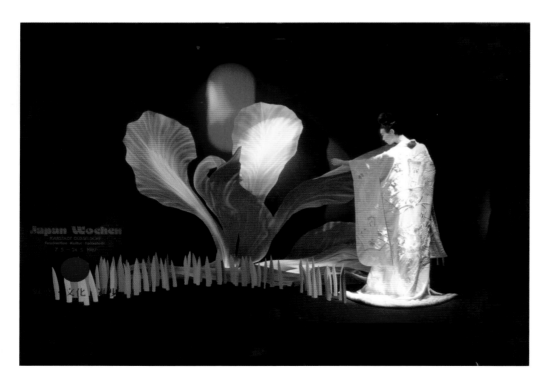

Building to Impress

PRECEDING PAGES
LEFT Caryatids above Macy's 34th Street entrance, Herald Square, New York City.
RIGHT The peacock, symbol of Daimaru, appears over the Osaka store's entrance. Evocations of past grandeur have traditionally been part of the architectural vocabulary of department stores. The caryatids could have just stepped off the Parthenon.

OPPOSITE The Egyptian Escalator in Harrods, known as the "stairway to heaven," designed in the 1990s by William Mitchell. This elaborate décor was commissioned by Harrods' former owner Mohamed Al-Fayed, who believed in enveloping shoppers with magic from the moment they entered.

BELOW An ornate and delicate imperial staircase dominates the center of the atrium in Printemps, 1907, tempting visitors upward through the store.

In the grand era of department-store construction at the end of the nineteenth century, stores were designed to dazzle shoppers with palatial luxury. Their impressive, monumental exteriors arrested the eye and promised an interior filled with good things. Once inside, the spectator's senses were overwhelmed by volumes of space and heaps of merchandise, as well as the fragrance of perfumes and the ceaseless hum of commerce. As Frantz Jourdain, architect of several of the Samaritaine's buildings in Paris, put it, a successful store exterior pulled people inside, while a good interior kept them from wanting to leave.[1]

Their effect on shoppers, whether city dwellers, provincials, suburbanites, or tourists, was magnetic. Department stores were adept at portraying themselves as travelers' destinations similar to yet distinct from monuments, public buildings, cathedrals, and palaces. When French architect Paul Sédille took on the project of designing a building for Printemps in 1881, he realized that the venture required the structure to be "marked on its exterior with features that command attention, and whose image would be carried home as a souvenir by the foreign or provincial visitor."[2] Indeed, department stores issued booklets, trade cards, and postcards on which their store appeared along with other famous stops on a standard grand tour itinerary. This tradition continued well into the twentieth century, as attested to by the 1930s booklet of scenes of the Vieux Carré issued by the D. H. Holmes store of New Orleans. By then tourists were quite accustomed to making a visit to a city's major department stores an essential part of their trip.[3]

It is worth noting that few people actually saw a department store as it was portrayed in images. In reality it was difficult, if not impossible, for a viewer to gain an inclusive perspective of the store from a pedestrian vantage point. Invariably, representations of stores dominated the landscape, obliterating competing buildings or anything that distracted from their hulking singularity. Also, if the image was an artist's conception, it usually presented the store as larger than real life, completely out of scale with the pedestrians, carriages, and trolleys passing by. An extreme example is an illustration of the Dufayel store in Paris in which the interior appears monstrously huge because shoppers are shown at about one-fourth actual size (see pages 20–21).[4]

Although their show windows revealed their true identities, the otherwise grand and imitative "veneer of classical forms" that dressed up department-store facades bore considerable resemblance to other monumental buildings.[5] Gigantic clocks and clock towers suggested that the site was a public building, as did the fact that many stores occupied entire city blocks. In Germany, department stores were designed to conform to dignified traditional building types

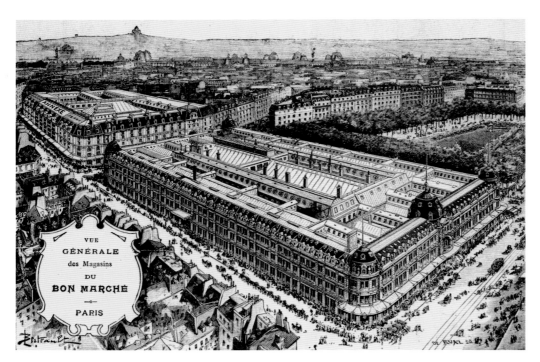

such as city halls and train stations. French department stores vied with palaces and the Parisian opera hall. The parades of confused shoppers who entered the Musée du Louvre and asked for the glove department can be forgiven for their faux pas. Indeed, the Grands Magasins du Louvre did not look so very different from the museum to the inattentive tourist's eye. The Leonhard Tietz store in Düsseldorf could also have been easily mistaken for a museum.[6]

Some of the confusion may have been caused by the sheer size of the stores, which were among the largest buildings lining major boulevards. The earliest stores were prone to horizontal growth as they took over neighboring storefronts one after another. As a result, a store sometimes lacked a unified appearance, but that would change once it gained financing to build a "palace." The Bon Marché in Paris and Stewart's in New York City were among the first, in the 1860s, to erect new buildings designed specifically to house a large retailing business. Stewart's opened a cast-iron building on Broadway near 10th Street in 1862. By the end of the decade it had been enlarged to four times its original size, presenting shoppers with a sales floor of 60,000 square feet (5,574 square meters), larger than a football field and almost four times the size of the New York Stock Exchange floor at its opening in 1903.[7] By the early 1880s, after more than a decade-long building program, the Bon Marché occupied more than 500,000 square feet (46,451 square meters), making it the world's largest retail store. "World's largest" was a title, however, that would alternate among contenders such as Marshall Field in Chicago, Wanamaker's in Philadelphia, Wertheim on Leipziger Strasse, Tietz on Alexanderplatz, and Macy's in Herald Square. It would be hazardous to guess which was, or is, the largest department store ever built, though Macy's held that title for most of the twentieth century with over 2,000,000 square feet (185,800 square meters).

The rising value of real estate in cities' commercial centers in the nineteenth century compelled stores upward, particularly in the United States, where, without the height restrictions imposed by European cities, the sky was the limit. Even in American cities where building height was regulated by law, it seemed that the ordinances were meant to yield to the onrush of commerce. In 1900 Marshall Field obtained permission from the Chicago city council to build a new twelve-story building on State Street, two stories higher than the city allowed. By 1907 the building would extend along the whole block. Wanamaker's new building, completed in 1911, was of the same height. These were not the highest: the Boston Store, in Chicago, reached seventeen stories, while Hudson's in Detroit exceeded twenty. Upper stories attracted few

LEFT Glass ceiling spanning Printemps' galleries, ca. 1906.

BELOW The interior of the Grands Magasins du Louvre presented a bright appearance in the atrium, but side galleries in the early department stores tended to be dark.

OPPOSITE Grand turn-of-the-century atrium and stairs in the Wertheim store in Leipziger Strasse, designed by Alfred Messel. The statue, symbolizing labor, is by Ludwig Manzel.

shoppers, so they were often occupied by administrative offices and workshops or were rented to other businesses. Conventional wisdom had it that any economic advantage deriving from a store's height ended at about nine stories.[8]

In Europe laws were less flexible. Parisian stores were not permitted to be taller than the width of the streets on which they were located. This led them to choose wide streets and to have a large footprint, or to spread out into more than one building.[9] Stringent fire laws in Germany limited stores to four or five floors, producing some truly huge footprints. In Berlin, the Hermann Tietz store, built on Alexanderplatz in 1911, had one facade measuring 800 feet (243.8 meters), and occupied an enormous area of at least 240,000 square feet (22,297 square meters). Each of its floors was larger than a super Wal-Mart store of today. The luxurious Wertheim store on Leipziger Strasse was quite vast as well, with over 150,000 square feet (13,935 square meters) per floor about this time (see pages 116–17).[10]

Stores in London also had height limits. Harry Selfridge was thwarted in his wish to build a twelve-story building in 1909, settling for five stories at the structure's tallest point, with selling space of little more than 250,000 square feet (23,226 square meters).[11] One of the challenges he had to meet in the construction phase was, he noted, "fifty-seven claims against us for proposed obstruction of daylight, which the law holds to be the property of adjoining realty owners and tenants." He, of course, had grown accustomed to the way his old employer, Marshall Field, virtually ruled Chicago when it came to getting permission to exceed height (and other) ordinances.[12]

However Gibraltar-like, permanent, and unchanging department stores seem in imagination, the truth is that they have always been in a constant state of change. This applies to all facets of their affairs but especially to their physical status. From their beginnings until after World War II, and in some cases longer, they grew ever larger. More recently, many have shrunk as departments are eliminated and floors are closed off. If a typical size for a major department store could be identified over decades of expansion and contraction, it might be from four to eight stories tall and range from 300,000 to 700,000 square feet (27,871 to 65,032 square meters). Historically, these parameters would encompass many present and past flagship stores such as Bloomingdale's, Harrods, KaDeWe, Woodward & Lothrop, Saks Fifth Avenue, Printemps, and most Japanese stores.

Beginning in the 1870s, the use of steel skeletons gave department stores a striking degree of interior openness and made expansive glass fronts possible. Paris stores gloried in open expanses,

OVERLEAF Large glass cupola in Galeries Lafayette, completed in 1912, displaying the Art Nouveau styling of architect Ferdinand Chanut.

unlike those in London, which were hampered by fire regulations requiring interior fire walls every 40 feet (12.2 meters). This regulation provided another frustration for Selfridge, who hoped to present London shoppers—who he felt had not experienced a truly modern department store prior to his arrival in 1909—with an open-plan store. Since the turn of the century, a store without inner walls had been considered a sign of modernity in the United States.[13]

Store interiors also gained a feeling of cathedral-like spaciousness from lofty skylights that admitted a flood of daylight. Without them it was impossible to illuminate large, deep buildings adequately. But even skylights were insufficient, as is evident in buildings such as the Bon Marché annex completed in 1923. Despite the large central skylight crowning its grand Art Deco hall, electric lights were needed to supplement the daylight.[14] And atriums had another drawback; they forfeited floor space. Thus it is surprising that they remained a design feature long after the widespread installation of electric lights. Was it because they demonstrated a store's size, busyness, and plan of organization at a glance? Or because facilitating the examination of goods by daylight seemed more honest? Or was it simply, as historians have argued, a "key component of seductive marketing strategies," an example of luxurious wastefulness that added value to the merchandise?[15]

Most nineteenth-century department stores had atriums. The Bon Marché boasted numerous small skylights, in addition to its large atrium, which exceeded 17,000 square feet (1,580 square meters), yet it failed to convey volume the way that Printemps would succeed in doing. After a devastating fire in 1881, Printemps was rebuilt with a single large atrium according to a design by architect Paul Sédille. The building became a model for the ideal department store and was imitated all over the world.[16] Its famed colored-glass ceiling was destroyed when floors were closed in the 1930s.[17]

Interior atriums were also common in stores in Germany, Japan, Canada, and other countries. Their use continued in large German stores until the Depression, when department-store construction came to a halt.[18] They were plentiful in cities throughout the United States as well until about World War I. An exception was Chicago, where few big stores besides Marshall Field had them. Eventually, the attitude toward atriums took a 180-degree turn. Pragmatic department-store designers of the post–World War II era would declare "intensely bright" ceilings of all sorts distractions from the shopper's "zone of interest," the merchandise.[19]

Another common feature of department-store architecture was the corner tower. Parisian stores had a pronounced preference for castlelike corner towers capped with domes, and they became

LEFT The monumental stairway in Mitsukoshi's Nihonbashi store, ca. 1914, along with the heavily ornamented and pillared galleries present the appearance of a building exterior.

RIGHT The thirteen-story north atrium of the Marshall Field store was designed by Charles Atwood.

OPPOSITE The rotunda of the City of Paris department store was reconstructed following San Francisco's earthquake and fires in 1906.

DENTELLES

OPPOSITE Detail of a mosaic at the Bon Marché indicating the Paris store's lace department and the monogram of its founder, Aristide Boucicaut.

RIGHT At the entrance to the Philadelphia John Wanamaker store, the founder's initials, rendered in his striking cursive style, were worked into the mosaic floor.

LEFT AND ABOVE The main atrium in Chicago's Marshall Field store, topped by the Tiffany Studios ceiling made of 1.6 million pieces of handmade glass, as seen on a postcard (left) and in a photograph (above). Louis Comfort Tiffany, director of the studios, was a leading American glass maker, jeweler, and lamp designer, whose father founded the jewelry firm on Fifth Avenue.

a hallmark of French department-store building style. Vestiges of towers can still be found today in stores worldwide, in some cases radically simplified as entrances sliced off on a diagonal angle. Other classic examples of corner towers have included Whiteleys in London and, most famously, Louis Sullivan's Carson Pirie Scott store in Chicago. Domed corner rotundas can also be seen on the Mitsukoshi Nihonbashi store's annex, and variations on the theme form part of the architecture of El Corte Inglés in Madrid and Barcelona, Mitsukoshi's Ginza store, and Galeria Kaufhof in Frankfurt. The Modernism of the 1920s and 1930s inspired the revival of rounded corners that hint at rotundas, represented in the Schocken store in Stuttgart as well as in American stores such as Maas Brothers in St. Petersburg, Florida, and Lichtenstein's in Corpus Christi, Texas. A number of stores, such as Anthony Hordern in Sydney, Australia, and the Wertheim store on Moritzplatz in Berlin, were built with dual or central towers, some outfitted with a clock. Among the weirder towers was that of the Daniels & Fisher store in Denver; modeled after the Campanile in Venice's St. Mark's Square, it rose some 330 feet (100 meters) into the air. Another tall tower, that of Bullocks Wilshire, topped with a blue-green light, was better integrated into the overall design.[20]

On the whole, however, American stores have tended to be devoid of towers and corner treatments, preferring rectangular warehouse-style buildings that, at their more elegant, feature granite facades fronted with columns or pilasters. As an English visitor once put it, apart from their show windows, American stores traditionally employed "factory architecture."[21] The same could be said of Canadian stores. Plain exteriors, such as Eaton's in Toronto and Winnipeg and Woodward's in Vancouver, reassured customers that the price they paid was not calculated to cover unnecessarily elegant trappings.[22]

A few leading American stores, however, opted for a more impressive Beaux-Arts architectural style. Marshall Field's, Wanamaker's in Philadelphia, Filene's, and B. Altman's on Fifth Avenue adopted princely buildings in the years before World War I, when American commerce "discovered art." Designed perhaps to convince the public that it was no tawdry bazaar, Altman's granite edifice of 1906 was described, somewhat sarcastically, as "that public library in dignity, that State Capitol in white impressiveness (see pages 26–27)."[23]

The architectural references and solidity of construction that characterize even ordinary department stores of the mid-twentieth century—as well as their use of premier materials inside and out—inspire appreciation when compared to the concrete-block, warehouse-type building techniques found so often in commercial construction today. However, department-store

buildings were not always admired in their own day, nor was it easy to discover a style appropriate to their purposes, being perpetually divided between functionalism and symbolism. One of the leading criticisms of department-store buildings has been that they are vulgar structures consisting of architectural elements chosen primarily to represent false luxury, a ploy that becomes nakedly obvious when the impression fails.

Thus, in 1874 the main atrium of the Bon Marché was regarded as unsuccessful in its attempt at loftiness because it was of "no great height"—its three upper-gallery ceilings were deemed too low.[24] Wanamaker's adapted freight terminal, which served as a department store until a new building was completed in 1911, had unusual Moorish towers and was judged "almost grotesque."[25] Germans so hated French department stores' "effusive ornament" that they adopted neo-Gothic styles that to their detractors marked a Germanic "triumph of the Kolossal" that was "heavy" and "overpowering."[26] Printemps, considered by some to be Paris's most successful example of department-store architecture, had gilded corner domes that a British critic in 1907 labeled "hideous mural advertisements."[27] Selfridges' 1909 building, designed by the esteemed Chicago architect Daniel Burnham, was ridiculed as "Franco-American Renaissance," with too-elaborate columns and detailing that "mocked the classic pretensions of the whole."[28] The Samaritaine's 1905 Art Nouveau architecture was regarded as a "blight on the neighborhood" and was the subject of "countless jokes" in the Paris press. City officials eventually prevailed over architect Frantz Jourdain's design; its glass domes and Art Nouveau ironwork were removed in the 1920s, and its colorful ceramic tile panels were stripped off in 1937. To lovers of Art Nouveau, the resulting renovation created a "severe" and "rather ponderous" Art Deco exterior.[29] The new Printemps store of the 1920s was a "cross between the Crystal Palace and the interior of the Opera" all under a "giddy dome."[30] When New York stores moved en masse to Fifth Avenue and built their "overgrown palaces," they were derided as false representations of the princely abodes of the Italian Renaissance; their "ornate pilasters" and "pretend" arcades were considered a symptom of the decade's mercenary "Artistic Awakening of Business," and at odds with the roaring traffic of the street.

Paradoxically, the very same stores that were roundly criticized were also praised, sometimes in the same breath. In the 1870s the Bon Marché drew gasps from shoppers viewing the frescoed ceiling of its reading room.[31] Art Nouveau was extremely popular at the turn of the century. This new art, known in Germany as Jugendstil, was inspired mainly by the organic shapes of the natural world, which it expressed in elaborate and decorative curvilinear forms. Artists

reflected this new art in everything from porcelain to architecture. Among the movement's leading protagonists were Gustav Klimt in painting, Alphonse Mucha in posters, René Lalique in glass and jewelry, and Antonio Gaudí in architecture. Whatever its excesses, it was viewed as innovative and honest in its use of structural steel and motifs drawn from nature rather than borrowed from the past. Jourdain's Samaritaine was seen as a "radically modern" building that expressed the unity of the arts through a collaboration of painters, sculptors, and other decorative artists.[32] L'Innovation in Brussels, of Art Nouveau design by Victor Horta, was viewed as "graceful" and "a refreshing oasis in a desert of commonplaceness."[33] German buildings, particularly the Wertheim store on Leipziger Strasse by celebrated architect Alfred Messel, were seen as "timeless" and hailed as "the harbinger of a new architecture."[34] KaDeWe was praised for its "uniform artistic design" without ostentation and for using "only genuine materials."[35] American stores were described as "light" and "airy," functional and modern, as well as practical in design because more stories could be added in the future.[36] Still, the Art Nouveau style was not prevalent in the United States, with the outstanding exception of Louis Sullivan's Schlesinger & Mayer department-store building in Chicago, completed in 1903 under the new Carson Pirie Scott ownership. Although hailed as being "as modern as the calendar itself," evidencing "nary a vestige of the past," Sullivan's building may have had greater influence abroad than on American department-store design.[37]

For better and for worse, it might be admitted that department-store architecture has always encompassed an advertisement for itself. What changes is the advertising message conveyed. Some buildings have been meant to communicate a no-nonsense message of thrift and bargains, whereas others have promised an orgy of exuberant consumption. Still others evoke trust, efficiency, progress, modernity, youthful stylishness, or traditionalism.

However frankly functional, patently overblown, or gorgeously stunning their exteriors, department stores are primarily about what is inside. Their interior monumentality has been expressed not only in high ceilings and atriums but also in wide aisles, mighty pillars, and grand staircases, many of which curved sinuously from floor to floor, making an especially showy sight on the ground floor, where they often began as dual staircases. As was true of corner rotundas, the art of the staircase was perfected in Paris before spreading across the globe.[38]

Nineteenth- and early-twentieth-century stores also pioneered profuse interior decoration of a style that continued to define luxury well into the twentieth century. The ornamentation included stair and gallery railings, decorated ceilings, murals, grillwork, ornately carved

PRECEDING PAGES The relatively unornamented facade of the Wertheim store on Leipziger Strasse in Berlin, 1898. Designed by architect Alfred Messel to be dignified and stylistically timeless, it stood in stark contrast to the neighboring Hermann Tietz store (see pages 102 and 103).

paneling, and elaborate light fixtures. Paris's Dufayel store (later, Bazar de l'Hôtel de Ville, or BHV) was one of the more rococo examples, despite its profile as a no-nonsense people's store. Inside it was gorgeously outfitted with a grand self-supporting curved staircase rising from the ground floor and a good share of the over two hundred statues that peppered the store inside and out.[39] The Berlin Hermann Tietz store on Alexanderplatz had pillars of Siena marble, glass mosaics, and marble balustrades among its "thousand and one luxurious details."[40] The early Bon Marché was among the stores with richly painted and ornamented ceilings, as was the lush Leonhard Tietz store in Elberfeld, Germany, designed by Wilhelm Kreis, Germany's leading department-store architect before World War I. Kreis also designed the Leonhard Tietz store in Cologne. The Tietz store in Düsseldorf, designed by Josef Maria Olbrich, an exponent of Austrian Art Nouveau, set a high standard for luxurious yet functional department-store architecture in Germany.[41] Marshall Field's six-story vaulted ceiling, composed of 1,600,000 pieces of handmade iridescent glass by Tiffany & Co., achieved worldwide recognition.[42] Many stores had chandeliers, but German stores, whose interiors were surprisingly luxurious, especially in contrast to their austere exteriors, featured intricate light fixtures of considerable originality, particularly the Wertheim stores and the Tietz stores in Düsseldorf and Elberfeld, which were fitted with metal filigree fixtures, arrays of small bulbs, and lights draped from swagged chains.[43] A popular theme found in many stores' murals, statuary, and external decorations has been the history of commerce. The Bon Marché of the 1870s displayed a bust of Jean-Baptiste Colbert, Louis XIV's minister of finance.[44] John Wanamaker commissioned two large stained-glass windows depicting financiers Stephen Girard and Robert Morris, as well as a bank, money scales, and money bags. German department stores built in the early twentieth century in Breslau, Mannheim, Wiesbaden, and other cities often sported immense rooftop globes girded by their store name and sometimes accompanied by a statue of Mercury, the god of trade and commerce. The most striking example of this type of ornament was found atop the Hermann Tietz store on Leipziger Strasse in Berlin, where the globe and associated statuary formed a top-heavy, Baroque counterpoint to the otherwise modern, all-glass storefront (see pages 102 and 103).[46]

The use of the steel frame in the construction of large buildings in the late nineteenth century immediately opened up possibilities for modern design that advanced functionality and dispensed with historicism and elaborate ornamentation. It also facilitated the development of Art Nouveau decorative treatments for both exteriors and interiors. The steel building

OPPOSITE Detail of the Art Nouveau facade of Galeries Lafayette, rue de la Chaussée-d'Antin, designed by Ferdinand Chanut and completed in 1912.

FAR LEFT Rue de Rivoli facade of the Samaritaine department store, by Frantz Jourdain, ca. 1912.

LEFT Frieze-like stylized Art Nouveau mural of flowers, peacocks, and ornamental trees, overlaid with cast-iron grill work in the grand hall of the Samaritaine department store.

technology was available in the 1880s, but it wasn't until the next decade that department stores began to be built with the new framing. William Le Baron Jenney's Second Leiter Building in Chicago, which opened as the Siegel-Cooper store in 1891, was the first such building on State Street, but neither it nor Marshall Field's steel-framed annex of 1893 displayed the all-glass fronts more commonly found in steel-frame stores in Germany in the 1890s, which featured unadorned fronts with big expanses of floor-to-ceiling glass on each floor, interrupted only by plain steel members.

The age of glass and exposed steel quickly came to an end in Germany after disastrous revelations of how poorly these materials stood up to fire.[47] This danger had become a reality in the fire that destroyed the new Simpson's store in Toronto in 1895. The solution for reducing the vulnerability of steel to heat was to cover it in fireproof material such as terra-cotta and concrete, as was done when Simpson's was rebuilt.[48] In the United States, building regulations required that steel framing be covered in fireproof materials.[49]

In France, the 1900 Paris Exposition inspired steel-and-glass department-store buildings decorated with Art Nouveau flourishes. Some of Paris's most notable department-store architecture and interior design was produced during the short ten-year period in which Art Nouveau reigned, including work at Galeries Lafayette, the Samaritaine, and Printemps. Jourdain had promoted Art Nouveau at the Exposition in his role as head of decorative arts, while René Binet, who would preside over the 1906–10 enlargement of Printemps, designed the entrance gate, Porte Monumentale, also known as La Porte Binet.[50]

Going Modern

The big Paris stores commanded the finest craftspeople of the time. In the rebuilding of Binet's Printemps in 1923, Louis Brière recreated the magnificent glass dome; it was removed for safekeeping during World War II and replaced in 1973. Édouard Schenck contributed graceful Art Nouveau designs in wrought iron to the Samaritaine, Magasins Réunis, and Galeries Lafayette, transitioning to Art Deco in his filigreed nameplate medallion for the facade of the new 1926–27 Samaritaine no. 3 on the rue de Rivoli and rue de Pont Neuf.

Art Nouveau and Art Deco co-existed for close to a decade. Art Deco took hold in the 1920s, its rigor and clean lines in sharp contrast to the decadent sinuousness of Art Nouveau. The apogee of Art Deco was the 1925 Exposition Internationale des Arts Décoratifs et Industriels Modernes in Paris. This exposition also affected department-store styling, in France and

ABOVE The Bon Marché's Pomone pavilion at the Paris exposition of decorative arts in 1925, designed by the son of Louis-Charles Boileau, Louis-Hippolyte Boileau.

LEFT Modern interpretation of Art Deco style by the architectural firm of Faure-Dujarric for Aux Trois Quartiers in Paris.

OPPOSITE Luxurious yet restrained Art Deco style of the Bon Marché annex, designed by Louis-Hippolyte Boileau in the 1920s.

PRECEDING PAGES
Hermann Sachs's "Spirit
of Transportation" fresco
in the automobile portico
of Bullock's Wilshire.

ABOVE AND RIGHT Two
views of the Art Deco
stairways in Printemps,
constructed after the
building was rebuilt in
1924 following a
catastrophic fire in 1921.
Known as "Escalier
d'Honneur," this stairway
begins in one of the four
rotundas located at each
corner of the store (right).

elsewhere. The exposition buildings housing Paris's four largest stores, the Bon Marché, Galeries Lafayette, Printemps, and the Samaritaine, introduced a new twentieth-century approach to luxury that made nineteenth-century styles look dated. At first, in the late 1920s, some stores adopted Art Deco's more opulent aspects, including the use of exotic materials and surface decoration. This is exemplified in the United States in buildings such as Stewart & Company on Fifth Avenue in New York (later Bonwit Teller) and Bullock's Wilshire in Los Angeles. During the Depression, however, great simplifications were made. Not only was the absence of decorative elements seen as more expressive of the machine age, but streamlined Moderne-style plainness suited Depression budgets because it was cheaper to produce. Lavish details such as the bronze doors and exotic imported woods used for paneling at Stewart's or the marble perfume galleries and designer rugs by artists such as Sonia Delaunay at Bullock's became a thing of the past. Stewart's, in fact, closed six months after its opening date, and not long after Bonwit Teller took it over the interior was remodeled.[51]

In Germany, modern architecture developed in a more severe mode that eventually rejected as "irrational" even minimal decorative elements. The Wertheim store on Leipziger Strasse by Alfred Messel, an architect known for both "distinguished simplicity and harmonious monumentality," was considered a model of impressive yet dignified commercial architecture.[52] The modern movement was encouraged by Grand Duke Ernst Ludwig von Hessen-Darmstadt, who helped promote aesthetic reform and launched the Darmstadt Artists' Colony with architects such as Joseph Maria Olbrich, a pupil of Otto Wagner, and Peter Behrens. Olbrich, co-founder of the Vienna Secession, designed a number of department stores, including the above-mentioned Leonhard Tietz store in Düsseldorf, which is now classified as a national monument. His student, Wilhelm Kreis, continued in the same vein, designing monumentalist buildings defined by exteriors of closely spaced, smooth vertical pilasters such as the Theodor Althoff store in Dortmund.[53]

In retrospect, few German department-store buildings seem as modern today as Erich Mendelsohn's three stores for the Schocken chain, in Nuremberg in 1925–26, Stuttgart in 1928, and Chemnitz in 1929. The Stuttgart store became a key building in Mendelsohn's career. Although it was a beautiful object that photographed well, the store's modeling after a factory rather than a palace was evidenced in a stark interior complemented by a presentation of goods that was almost puritanical in its regimentation.[54] Mendelsohn's use of ribbon windows proved to be very influential, although not all architects used them as functionally as he did. Rather than adopt a steel-supported, all-glass facade, he walled the lower portion of the windows so that the interior shelving fixtures could be mounted against the exterior walls. Above the fixture walls on each floor was a continuous strip of windows. The arrangement permitted light to enter without sacrificing badly needed merchandise display and storage space. No doubt he was aware of how messy the all-glass-and-steel stores of the early twentieth century, such as the Samaritaine and the Grand Bazar on rue de Rennes in Paris, Schmoller in Frankfurt, and Kander in Mannheim, could look when merchandise was placed near the windows.[55]

Mendelsohn's influence was widespread, especially in Germany, where a number of stores were inspired by his designs. The Hermann Tietz store on Chausseestrasse in Berlin was designed by KaDeWe architect Johann Emil Schaudt with a stairway tower similar to Schocken's Stuttgart store.[56] Others included the Wertheim store in Breslau by Hermann Dernburg, the Leonhard Tietz store in Solingen, and the Breuninger department store in Stuttgart.[57]

Mendelsohn's architecture was also respected by modernists in Japan, such as Kikuji Ishimoto, who studied with Walter Gropius at the Bauhaus in 1922. In 1928 Ishimoto designed a building for Shirokiya in Tokyo in the International style. Its horizontal bands of windows created an effect similar to that of the glass stairwell in Mendelsohn's Stuttgart Schocken store.[58]

In Germany, the massive Karstadt store on Berlin's Hermannplatz, its towers lit dramatically at night,[59] opened in 1929 and ushered in a style of monumental streamlined modernism that would become popular in the 1930s. One of the last German department stores to feature an atrium,[60] it was designed by Philip Schäfer and inspired by pre–World War I design competition entries by Peter Behrens, Adolf Loos, and Franz Amelung.[61] Adolf Hitler, after landing at the Tempelhof airport in 1934, declared that Karstadt was the only building in Berlin that struck his eye from the air and that the city's public buildings must become equally impressive.[62]

Stores such as Peter Jones in London, Wieboldt's in Oak Park, Illinois, and Coulter's in Los Angeles adopted similar moderne stylings. Peter Jones was first to introduce show windows uninterrupted by vertical supports, the continuity of which was limited only by the maximum width of the glass panels themselves, all made possible by an enormous horizontal steel beam above the windows.[63]

By the mid-1930s the public began to adjust to the odd sight of department stores with a narrow ribbon of windows above the first floor—or no windows at all. This design, which frankly acknowledged that the department store was an artificially controlled environment, was, of

Modernism, stripped of the minimal ornamentation of the Art Deco 1920s, dominated department-store buildings in the 1930s. Shown here, clockwise from top right, are: Hermann Dernburg's Wertheim store, built in what was then Breslau, Germany (Wrocław, Poland, today); Erich Mendelsohn's Schocken store in Stuttgart; the Peter Jones store in London, by William Crabtree; interior stairway of Tokyo's Shirokiya; Erich Mendelsohn's Schocken store in Chemnitz; and Berlin's enormous Karstadt store.

OVERLEAF The Shirokiya department store in Tokyo was the work of Bauhaus-trained architect Kikuji Ishimoto, 1927.

Stuttgart. Schocken-Bau

PETER JONES

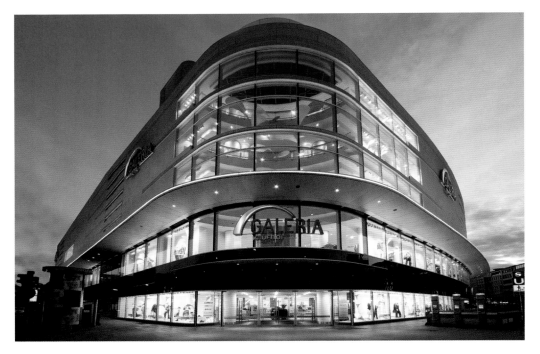

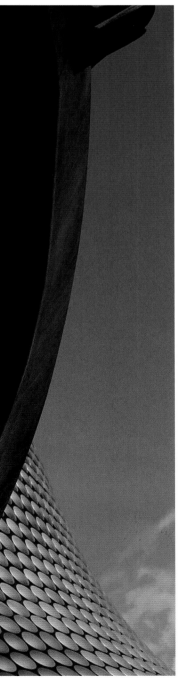

Whether with glass, filigree, or futuristic materials, department stores built in recent years continue to function as attention grabbers. Galeria Kaufhof in Frankfurt, Germany (top far left); John Lewis at night, Leicester, England (top left); Selfridge's in Birmingham, England (bottom left); and John Lewis, Leicester, by day (right).

course, a recognition that windows were unnecessary (even liabilities because of sun damage and humidity), thanks to improved artificial light and full air conditioning.[64] A different style of "windowless" store, à la the triumphal modernism of Karstadt, was represented by the stunning but never completed 1930s exterior remodeling of Galeries Lafayette by Pierre Patout, designer of the *Normandie*. It featured dramatic protruding vertical bays of glass that suggested smokestacks on an ocean liner, a vessel supplying the perfect metaphor for the department store as a self-sufficient city-within-a-city.[65]

The rational approach to architecture taken by Mendelsohn but not fully realized in the Schocken stores dominated American department-store design after the war. A foremost exponent, Louis Parnes, whose *Planning Stores That Pay* was published in 1948, bluntly stated the principles of the new approach, which rejected almost every feature that had once characterized grand department stores. Stores were to be, paraphrasing Le Corbusier, "machines for selling." Typical exteriors of the past, he stated, resembled nothing but warehouses with "pompous and boastful facades and interior columns to attract and impress the masses." They contributed nothing to make store operation more efficient or less costly. The penchant for chandeliers and elegant light fixtures was misplaced, according to this view, because they attracted the eye, whereas modern lighting emphasized the light itself and engineered it to keep the shopper's gaze riveted on the merchandise. Overly wide aisles wasted space better used for displays, ignoring precise calculations that had been developed specifying how much space was needed by customers to move through the store and examine the merchandise. Elevators and central staircases, however beautiful the latter, should be replaced by escalators, which could carry far more people. Foley's, built in Houston in 1948 with an interior designed by Raymond Loewy Associates, provided a prime example of an efficient, windowless store designed to facilitate sales and circulate stock and customers without impediment.[66]

Others were in full agreement with Parnes that "as a machine for producing customers and distributing goods, the department store, like its counterpart in industry, should be based on sound theory and scientific observations."[67] Long, straight aisles, once the pride of stores such as Marshall Field, made no sense from this viewpoint. Modernists suggested that aisles should be no longer than 170 feet (52 meters), the longest distance from which a shopper could "distinguish a cup and saucer." Unless aisles permitted shoppers to view the merchandise in a meaningful way, what was the point?[68] Curved aisles were better than straight ones anyway, because curves required shoppers to view more merchandise as they wound their way around. In the words of architect Morris Lapidus, modern stores were planned "to guide consumers to the best selling locations by subtle suggestions in the

form of tricks in design, displays, lighting effects . . . that 'hypnotize' the shopper into going where the retailer wants him to go."[69]

Finally, one of the department store's most basic physical characteristics, its monumental size, came under scrutiny. Customers complained that it took them too long to find what they wanted. They felt their time was being wasted. A warning spread, alerting stores that their "sheer size" was no longer an asset in and of itself: "Unless space and facilities are provided for rest and relaxation in large stores, and unless there is variety in fixtures and arrangement to break up huge expanses of selling floor, weary shoppers will find relief in small establishments," experts cautioned. Beware too, they said, of large, empty spaces like overly generous aisles or elevator approaches "that may suggest slack business."[70] Vast spaces were valuable only if they were filled with vast crowds. Without them, they became a distinct liability.

Under the influence of the new modernism, with its revised concepts of rationality, the former Schocken store designed by Erich Mendelsohn in Stuttgart was razed in 1959. Although leading architects throughout the world declared it a pillar of modern architecture and tried to save it, its owners said its interior was hopelessly outdated.[71]

Despite the constraints department stores faced in the late twentieth century, the years around the turn of the new millennium did not mark the end of store construction in urban settings, but instead seemed to inspire several buildings of rich architectural interest. They often carried with them high expectations. The fortunes of a new store might rest not only on its parent store's reputation but equally on its ability to restore or revitalize a flagging commercial zone. Two new stores in England are located in depressed urban centers in the industrial Midlands. In the case of Galeries Lafayette in Berlin and Galeria Kaufhof in Chemnitz, the building sites are in the former East Germany.

Selfridges in Birmingham, England, opened in 2003 in a playfully biomorphic building with a rounded shape that almost defies description and has variously been called a blob, a flowing curve, and "unalloyed architectural entertainment." Inspired by 1960s chain-mail-like gowns by Paco Rabanne, the building was designed by the firm Future Systems, headed by the late Jan Kaplický and Amanda Levete. The four-story building's roof and walls are one continuous surface, and the entire facade is covered with 15,000 aluminum disks. The interior is dominated by dramatic crisscrossing escalator wells enclosed in smooth white casings. [72]

The John Lewis store in Leicester, England, represents the return of the glass facade of early-twentieth-century department stores. Opened in 2008, John Lewis is a glass box covered with

PRECEDING PAGES Carrying the all-glass-facade department stores of 1900 to a further extreme, the Galeria Kaufhof in Chemnitz, by Helmut Jahn, 2002, turns the building into a transparent case for merchandise.

BELOW A historic wrought-iron gate has been reinstalled at the entrance to KaDeWe in Berlin, under a contemporary glass canopy.

OPPOSITE, TOP A modern interpretation of the department store's historical elements of corner tower, dome, display windows, and massed volume mark the Berlin branch of Galeries Lafayette, designed by Jean Nouvel, 1996.

OPPOSITE, BOTTOM Gazing downward into the glass funnel inside Berlin's Galeries Lafayette gives onlookers a vertigo-inducing sense of a circular stairwell.

PRECEDING PAGES Exposed elevators, conceived of as a startling innovation when René Binet installed them in Printemps, continue to give consumers a box seat for the show of merchandise in KaDeWe one hundred years later.

TOP Over a hundred years old, Myer's in Melbourne has renovated part of its Bourke Street flagship store with a dramatic modern design by the firm NH Architecture that communicates youthfulness and joy.

ABOVE The perfume department in Myer's occupies the center of the store's new atrium.

RIGHT Light from a huge skylight in the renovated Myer's store picks up color in reflective bands on escalator wells.

OPPOSITE Blending Art
Nouveau curves with Art
Deco sensibilities, the new
Barneys New York in
Chicago, 2009, is the work
of architect Jeffrey
Hutchison.

ABOVE The new Barneys
on Oak Street in Chicago
features metal sculpture
and architectural
elements by John-Paul
Philippé.

BELOW Exterior, Barneys
New York in Chicago,
which presents a
contemporary adaptation
of the characteristic
department-store-building
format as found in Louis
Sullivan's iconic Carson
Pirie Scott building.

two layers of aluminum "lace" (adapted from historic textile designs), which permit light to enter while screening the building from exterior views. Winner of a Royal Institute of British Architects award, it is the work of Farshid Moussavi and Alejandro Zaera Polo, partners of Foreign Office Architects.[73]

Two other new glass stores also have interesting historical resonances. Jean Nouvel's Berlin building for Galeries Lafayette not only provides a visual interpretation of the Paris flagship store but also implies much more. Given the significance of Kristallnacht, when National Socialists smashed windows in Jewish-owned department stores, synagogues, and other buildings in 1938, an all-glass department store in Berlin makes a historic statement whether intended or not. The store's interior features inverted glass cones that are updated versions of traditional atriums found in Paris stores. They tease shoppers who invariably wonder what happens if something is dropped into them. When he won the Pritzker Architecture Prize in 2008, Nouvel was hailed for his "exuberance" and "creative imagination," qualities borne out by the Berlin building.[74]

Galeria Kaufhof in Chemnitz, designed by Helmut Jahn, was completed in 2002, replacing the Kaufhof store that had occupied the building originally built for Schocken by Erich Mendelsohn. The Mendelsohn building, completed in 1930, will become an archaeological institute, while the new glass store, with its large, cantilevered canopies, does business near the train station in the city's center, radiating luminously against the night sky.[75]

Getting Attention

early everything department stores did could be considered advertising. As is true for celebrities, fame engenders fame. In the case of department stores, the public was prone to believe that if a store's name was familiar, it must be trustworthy and possess some special qualities.[1] To attract hordes of customers and win their good will, department stores did everything in their power to keep their names before the public. As the department-store industry developed, heavy advertising became one of its primary activities.

Like other shopping practices and ways of doing business introduced by department stores, advertising had not always been a common or approved activity in the mercantile world. Indeed, it had once been considered an undignified and improper means of encroaching on other tradesmen's territory. Before the development of mass production, when craftspeople made and sold their own work, the proprietor's reputation and personal communications were the main source of information about the quality of his goods.[2] Announcements in newspapers were just that, bare notices that goods were for sale at a certain place. When John Wanamaker set up shop with a men's and boys' clothing store in Philadelphia in 1861, the old ways were still dominant. "Really, it wasn't considered polite then to advertise," recalled a veteran merchant.[3] Nonetheless, Wanamaker persisted and became prominent among the new-thinking merchants who changed conventional attitudes toward advertising until his name became virtually synonymous with progress in the new field of advertising. "John Wanamaker as an advertiser," wrote an observer in 1893, "is talked about more than any other living man in America to-day."[4]

Advertising Wonders

The types of advertising that department stores have used are nearly endless. They encompass trinkets; posters, banners, and signs affixed to any stationary or moving surface imaginable; printed pieces such as postcards, catalogs, and mailers; and full use of the media either on a paid basis or as news and feature stories generated by activities and events staged by the stores. Distributing trinkets was one of the earliest methods department stores employed to spread their name and build good will. It's hard to imagine what a sensation the Grands Magasins du Louvre created when it began to give out balloons imprinted with the store's name in red or blue. The idea was quickly copied by other Paris stores, including the Coin de Rue.[5] The balloon giveaway took place in the 1870s, when the world was in the grips of a depression and rumors spread that the Louvre would close, possibly explaining the motive for the promotion. That same year other large Paris stores, including the Bon Marché, Petit Saint-Thomas, and Printemps began dis-

TOP Trade card with illustration by Felix Lorioux showing the famous red balloon given away by the Grands Magasins du Louvre.

ABOVE Beachgoers sit under an umbrella advertising New York City's Siegel-Cooper store.

WANAMAKER & BROWN,
The Largest Clothing House.
SIXTH & MARKET STS., PHILADELPHIA.

Trade card from Wanamaker & Brown, Philadelphia, also known as Oak Hall. By 1871 it was the largest men's clothing store in the country.

TOP AND ABOVE Trade cards from the John Wanamaker men's clothing store in Philadelphia, predecessor to his department store, and from the Shirokiya silk store in Tokyo.

OPPOSITE Galeries Lafayette fans, 1920s and 1930s. Paper fans provided an excellent advertising medium for early department stores, which, prior to air conditioning, were often so hot inside that customers fainted.

N. Israel   Album 1914   Berlin C

Januar

1 Donnerst.	Neujahr	
2 Freitag	Abel, Seth	
3 Sonnabd.	Enoch, Daniel	
4 Sonntag	n. Neuj. ☽	
5 Montag	Simeon	
6 Dienstag	H. 3 Könige	
7 Mittwoch	Melchior	
8 Donnerst.	Balthasar	
9 Freitag	Kaspar	
10 Sonnabd.	Paulus Eins.	
11 Sonntag	1. n. Ep. Erh.	
12 Montag	Reinhold ☿	
13 Dienstag	Hilarius	
14 Mittwoch	Felix	
15 Donnerst.	Habakuk	
16 Freitag	Marcellus	
17 Sonnabd.	Antonius	
18 Sonntag	2. n. Ep.	
19 Montag		
20 Dienstag		

5

12

13

Le Printemps

L'Été

AGENDA
ALMANACH
des
GRANDS MAGASINS du
LOUVRE

pour l'année
1925

RUE DE RIVOLI ET PLACE DU PALAIS-ROYAL
TÉLÉPHONE { LOUVRE 59-40 à 59-55
INTER SPECIAL 4-86 à 2-22
jours fériés et après fermeture
GUTENBERG 38-54

L'Automne

L'Hiver

Christmas 1954

Fall 1961

Fall 1963

1970–1979

Fall 1970

Spring 1971

1975–1980

Fall 1975

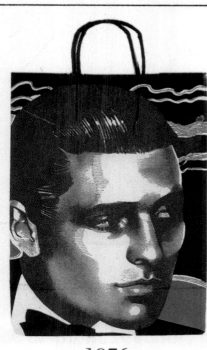

1976

PRECEDING PAGES
Date books and children's storybooks were often given as department-store souvenirs in the 1920s. The assemblage includes items from the Grands Magasins du Louvre, Nathan Israel, Galeries Lafayette, John Wanamaker, and other stores. The Klein's coupons were likely given as change for scrip payment during the Depression.

tributing premiums such as recipe and appointment books, bunches of violets (Printemps, naturally), and small toys.[6] Trade cards from the Bon Marché in Paris showed illustrations of comets, magic carpets, and sultans, with the implication that the store, too, was a wonder of the world.[7] Many stores in succeeding decades, including Sydney's David Jones and Eaton's in Canada, would hand out trade cards, which were collected by scrapbookers, and paper fans, which were badly needed in department stores before air conditioning.[8] Postcards succeeded trade cards. On them, buildings often appear huge and are shown from a perspective that emphasizes their breadth or height, their size and solidity suggesting prosperity and worthiness. Often buildings are depicted from a bird's-eye view, revealing a sprawling complex that seems to dominate the cityscape.[9]

Other objects were equally good at conveying the store's name and message. In the early twentieth century Mitsukoshi presented customers with umbrellas printed with the store name in large letters.[10] Selfridges distributed silver key charms to American customers as reminders to return on future trips, and bunches of shamrocks on St. Patrick's Day.[11] In more recent times, Bloomingdale's decorated shopping bags—initiated in 1954 with a design featuring a gloved hand, an umbrella, a rose, and a sheet of paper with a script B—continued the trinket-giving tradition.[12] In general, the practice of giving out shopping bags had an ulterior motive—to encourage shoppers to take their purchases with them, thus reducing deliveries.

Outdoor advertising has long been another common practice of department stores. Their own buildings have taken a leading role: storefronts have served as stages for promotional events, ledges as platforms for fashion shows, balconies as stands for speakers, and walls as surfaces against which to prop a ladder for Santa Claus. Around the turn of the last century, stores themselves frequently functioned as billboards. Each story would be outfitted with horizontal bands of signage indicating the store's major departments. Galeries Lafayette, for instance, bore so many signs on its front facade in 1906 that the building itself was all but obscured. As if that weren't enough for the eye to take in, large illuminated letters spelling out the store's name marched along the roofline, and between the windows on all four floors columns of block letters listed additional products sold in the store.[13] Exterior walls have also been used as canvases for paintings, such as the giant Mona Lisa that adorned the shutters of a Seibu store in Tokyo in the 1970s to call attention to the opening of its new art museum.[14]

Flags or banners, often stretching over several stories, have been liberally used to announce events or display fashions. As early as 1910 Mitsukoshi strung banners over its entrance to make daily announcements or welcome important visitors, such as William Howard Taft when he was U.S.

EMPIRE ··· SOUTHAMPTON · HULL · LEITH · PLYMOUTH · DOVER · FOLKESTONE · PORTSMOUTH · GIBRALTAR · VALETTA · QUEENSTOWN · ACCRA ·

SOUTH AFRICA

secretary of war.[15] The British loathed metaphorically "draping one's business in the flag," but in the U.S. it was well accepted to do so, even literally. Hudson's was not the only American store to display the Stars and Stripes on a gigantic flag strung across its exterior. Defying British custom, Selfridge spent huge sums decorating his exterior for the coronation of George VI.[16]

Lighting has also been used to great effect. Spotlights on roofs signaled a store's presence for miles, a technique that was especially effective when electricity was not yet universal, such as at Maison Dufayel in Paris about 1900.[17] Holidays and store anniversaries have long been celebrated with elaborate illumination. Exterior lighting might be designed to mimic lace or a jeweled necklace, or to create a scene such as a winter wonderland. Before Christmas in 1927 crowds of spectators blocked traffic to get a view of all eight stories of the Grands Magasins du Louvre, which had been turned into an Alpine panorama, complete with figures moving about building a snowman, an effect created by lighting and extinguishing thousands of bulbs.[18]

Before newspaper advertising became widespread in the late nineteenth century, other forms of outdoor advertising were commonly used, including posters, billboards, and electric and painted signs. John Wanamaker plastered his name all over Philadelphia when he began advertising his clothing store in the 1860s. He was regarded as either a hero or a devil, depending on the viewer's attitude. In 1870 an ambivalent admirer remarked that "the universal 'Wanamaker & Brown' [was] chiseled on the street crossings, painted on rocks, and mounted on house-tops. That they have not been wafted to the clouds, and tied to the tail of a fiery comet, is only because Yankee ingenuity has not yet devised the ways and means."[19] Wanamaker also erected thirteen billboards over 100 feet (30.5 meters) long.[20] Although billboards fell into disuse as newspaper advertising came to the fore, Bullock's in Los Angeles continued to use them into the 1940s, with the slogan, "If she really cares... it's from Bullock's."[21] In 1908 Mitsukoshi caught the attention of Japan by mounting a billboard atop Mount Fuji proclaiming it was "Japan's Number One."[22] Selfridge's 1909 store-opening advertising blitzkrieg was intense and earned him the moniker "Yankee bounder" for all the signs plastered on walls of the Underground and painted on London buses, asking, "Why Not Spend the Day at Selfridges?"[23] Perhaps even more blatant was the the Samaritaine's mode of outdoor advertising before Christmas 1927, when loudspeakers on every corner blared out messages such as, "Our clothing department is offering wonderful values in children's garments."[24]

Some outdoor advertising defaces the landscape, but posters usually have the virtue of being artistically engaging. Department stores called upon many of the best graphic artists of France, Japan, Germany, England, the United States, and other countries to produce posters. Taking advantage

PRECEDING PAGES

For very special occasions, an entire storefront can be turned into a kind of signboard, as occurred at Selfridges in London for the coronation of George VI in May 1937.

Dressed gaily in holiday lights, department stores enliven city streetscapes: Harrods (opposite); Galeries Lafayette (above); Saks Fifth Avenue in New York City (right). Saks is directly opposite Rockefeller Center, whose enormous tree complements Saks' spectacular decoration.

OPPOSITE Illustration by Hisui Sugiura for Mitsukoshi publicity in 1914.

RIGHT Most department stores of the mid-20th century staffed their own sign-making department to produce a prodigious volume of signs. Here Doris Lindholm works on a job for Stockholm's Nordiska Kompaniet.

TOP Photograph of Mitsukoshi's "brain trust," who provided illustrations and articles on culture and style for the store's magazine *Jiko,* ca. 1905.

ABOVE La Rinascente poster by Swiss graphic artist Max Huber, ca. 1951.

of improvements in color printing techniques, master lithographer Jules Chéret advanced the medium in Paris, making colored posters a favorite advertising method often found in Metro stations.[25] In Japan, as far back as 1899, posters of beautiful women wearing kimonos appeared in dozens of train stations throughout the country as an advertisement for Mitsukoshi.[26] The "beauty pictures" of Goyō Hashiguchi and Saburosuke Okada became a popular genre in Japan, and Okada's painting *Portrait of a Lady* furnished the basis for a Mitsukoshi poster in 1907. Before World War I Mitsukoshi hired one of the country's most talented illustrators, Hisui Sugiura, to head its new design department. His poster work, which integrated type into the design, featured Western styles such as Art Nouveau.[27] In Paris in 1910, posters by René Prejelan introduced men to the idea of buying ready-made suits in department stores.[28] Wanamaker's used artwork by French Post-Impressionist André Derain and linocuts by Olive Brinsmead to advertise August sales and special events.[29] Posters often had a second life in miniature as stamps for collectors.

The staff of department-store advertising departments could number as many as several hundred people, as was the case in Macy's Herald Square store in the late 1940s.[30] Many of the writers and editors went on to join or create advertising agencies outside the stores. In fact, as far back as the 1880s, Wanamaker's was instrumental in putting the N. W. Ayer agency, which placed its newspaper advertisements, on a solid footing.[31] Frequently, designers and illustrators were also on the stores' payrolls. Before World War I, when many functions were still performed in-house, some stores even printed their own mailers and catalogs and set type for their newspaper advertisements. The Schocken chain, though far from the largest or most fashionable department stores in Germany, had a design staff of Bauhaus-trained artists in the 1920s. László Moholy-Nagy and Herbert Beyer designed advertisements, signs, brochures, and posters. All of the store's printed pieces, from labels to letterheads and invoices, used Bauhaus-style typography. The store's advertising mailers were so chic that Salman Schocken considered them "miniature artworks."[32] La Rinascente, a firm that places particular emphasis on design, continued to maintain a design staff to turn out packaging materials, displays, and advertisements well after most stores had farmed out this expensive work.[33]

Catalogs often went beyond simply describing and illustrating items for sale, becoming fashion and literary magazines as well. In Britain at the turn of the twentieth century catalogs were the major form of advertising. Women treasured the Harrods and Dickins & Jones catalogs "as valuable presents, and would not part with them under any consideration."[34] The Wanamaker's fashion catalogs of the 1890s contained many illustrations in color.[35] Each fall the store also produced

Constructivist poster by Vladimir Mayakovsky and Aleksandr Rodchenko for GUM in the early 1920s advertising Moser pocket watches for orderly and businesslike people.

Poster for the Swiss chain Globus by Peter Birkhäuser in 1942, reading "Those who calculate, shop at Globus."

OPPOSITE Poster by Marcello Dudovich for travel luggage at La Rinascente, 1925.

a hundred-page book catalog featuring more than eight thousand titles. Paris department stores prided themselves on the artistry of their catalog covers, which were suitable for framing. A 1910 Printemps cover showing the eternal female as queen of the arts with merchants laying before her the earth's treasures was said to create "a true revolution in the art of catalogue production."[36]

Mitsukoshi, which would adopt the famous slogan "Today the Imperial Theatre; tomorrow Mitsukoshi," took its cultural mission very seriously.[37] In 1905 the store assembled a "brain trust" to advise on matters of fashion and culture. It comprised the country's leading artists and intellectuals, most of whom had traveled extensively or been educated in Western countries. The group, which came to be known as the Jikō Club, included important figures in Japan's modernization such as journalist Fukuchi Gen'ichiro, educator Nitobe Inazō, folklorist Yanagita Kunio, and artist Kuroda Seiki.[38] The store incorporated the group's research, thoughts, and words into a fashion journal that could run up to two hundred pages and include portraits of famous men and articles on art, travel, and nature.[39] Although the journal was intended in part to sell products, its primary purpose was to "project an image of Mitsukoshi as a source of fashion concepts that were dynamic, creative, and refined."[40]

In roughly the same period, premier American stores such as Wanamaker's and Marshall Field's began to publish their own fashion magazines. Wanamaker launched *La Dernière Heure à Paris* in 1909 and Marshall Field's similarly titled *Fashions of the Hour* appeared in 1914.[41] Some stores also published children's magazines, though self-published examples were soon replaced by syndicated versions that simply added the store's name to the cover.

With technological advances that lowered the cost of printing in the mid-1880s, newspapers became cheaper and readership increased dramatically, which made them attractive advertising vehicles.[42] French stores formed publicity departments and began to take out full-page advertisements. Pierre Giffard, *Figaro* journalist and author of *Les Grands bazars*, commented in 1882 that the big stores had "spurred the growth of advertising in the last twenty years."[43] By 1884 the Louvre was spending two million francs annually on advertising, buying "a whole page in every newspaper in the country" for special expositions of merchandise.[44] In Australia, David Jones began to take "bold, large advertisements" in Sydney and regional dailies.[45] So eager were newspapers for the business of department stores that novelist Émile Zola received a solicitation from a German newspaper peddling "the advantages of trans-Rhenean publicity for the sale of... merchandise" at his new department store, "Au Bonheur des Dames." As well known as Zola's book was, it's surprising that no one had really adopted that name for their store—and not entirely certain that they didn't.[46]

Department-store catalogs and magazines usually featured women on their covers, as demonstrated in the selection on these pages: charming illustration from Mitsukoshi's magazine, 1917 (above); cover of Nordiska Kompaniet Spring 1928 catalog, Stockholm (far left); 1930 cover of Karstadt magazine, illustrated by J. von Trost-Regnard (left); and stack of 1914 Printemps catalogs meant for customers living in French colonies (opposite).

Au Printemps

Modes
Fleurs
Plumes
Soieries
Lainages

GRANDE QUINZAINE

2ᵉ JOURNÉE

DU JEUDI 26
AU SAMEDI 28

MARS

1914

outre-mer Nᵒ 2.
Français
1914.

OPPOSITE Nordiska Kompaniet advertisement of 1916 with rhyming copy about Baron Per Fekt, who acquires his elegant wardrobe at the department store.

BELOW Advertisement for Paris's Belle Jardinière clothing store, showing the store and the Pont Neuf.

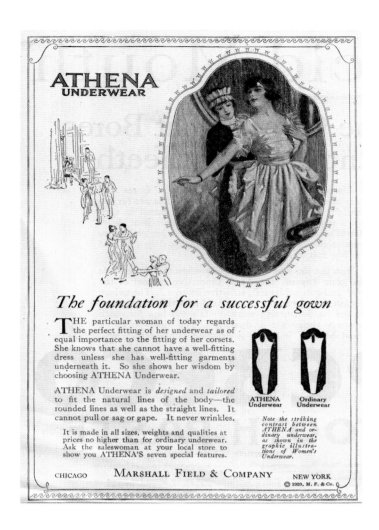

LEFT As did NK (opposite), Marshall Field suggests that its patrons are among the elite in this advertisement for foundation garments, ca. 1910.

ABOVE John Wanamaker advertised widely, including in his own publication, *Everybody's Magazine*.

Several department-store owners of this era became publishers of newspapers, including John Wanamaker, who bought *The North American*, and Jules Jaluzot of Printemps, who acquired *La Presse* and *La Patrie*, papers known for their nationalistic brand of patriotism.[47] But most stores merely bought advertising space. The amount of ad space started to increase in the 1890s and grew even greater after more papers began to publish Sunday editions around the turn of the century.[48] In 1893 Wanamaker's was running daily advertisements in some one hundred newspapers and weekly ads in about three hundred, paying more for advertising than any store in America, perhaps the world.[49] Seven major department stores in Chicago ran full-page newspaper advertisements every Sunday in the *Tribune*, while an evening newspaper filled twenty pages with their advertisements each Thursday in anticipation of Friday sales.[50] Meanwhile, Eaton's in Toronto made a deal for cut rates with the *Evening Star* in exchange for advertising exclusively in that paper. The arrangement was believed to have saved the struggling paper, as it "was actually bought for this advertisement," which always appeared on the back page.[51]

By the turn of the twentieth century, perhaps the only country in which department stores did relatively little newspaper advertising was Germany. Bazaar-type stores, out of which some department stores developed, were known for advertising that contained deceptive statements, or so critics claimed. To put the criticism in context, note that conservative German critics were also contemptuous of John Wanamaker (popularly regarded as a saint in the U.S.), whom they perceived as deviously skillful in bestowing his advertisements with "a certain 'biedermännisch' [middle-class] patina."[52] In an effort to protect themselves from criticism, German department stores that wished to entice middle-class customers avoided assertive or flamboyant statements, limiting their ads to lists of items for sale.[53] In the early twentieth century laws were enacted that penalized false and misleading advertising, and lawyers for the association of small shopkeepers carefully monitored department-store advertisements.[54]

Such laws would have crippled department-store advertising in the United States, where inflated claims were commonplace. American department-store advertising had its critics, but they were not able to leverage sufficient antagonism toward big stores to enact successful legislation against them. Rather, wise consumers soon learned to discount fabulous claims and to understand that the better stores avoided this kind of advertising. However, an incident with Wanamaker's shows how closely a store's enemies—in this case a store owner's political enemies—read advertisements. In 1893 Wanamaker's ran an ad for the dullest of merchandise, cambric corset covers, muslin "drawers," and loose-fitting "Mother Hubbard" nightgowns. The copy for these items stated: "Thoughts from Paris and our own best thoughts have been sewed into our Muslin Underwear . . . American women are very appreciative, and the demand now upon us proves that we are pleasing and serving them well."[55] For years afterward, Wanamaker's was ridiculed in the press with comments to the effect that the "good people of the Quaker City" didn't want any Paris thoughts or "frisky capers" in women's underwear.[56]

Japanese stores showed a special facility for getting attention with newspaper advertisements. Grasping the power of the void, Mitsukoshi ran an advertisement in 1906 that consisted of a large block of blank white space except for a brief notice that its ad would appear there the following day.[57] In 1910 the store ran a full-page advertisement in more than four hundred newspapers announcing its transformation from a dry goods store into a full department store. This act inspired other large stores in Japan to use newspaper advertising, which made sense in a country with high levels of literacy and newspaper readership.[58]

English stores did little newspaper advertising until Selfridge came on the scene. One of the reasons he chose London as the site for his store was, as he said, "the possibility of being able to address more than 5,000,000 people every morning through the newspapers within the metropolitan limits, and 20,000,000 outside."[59] Curiously, he had chosen to operate in an environment hostile to his showman style of merchandising and advertising, reprising his early struggles at Marshall Field's. After he left Field's in 1904, his successor had tried to reduce the advertising budget and restore dignity.[60] In London Selfridge found himself in an even more conservative milieu, but he evidently thrived on opposition. Prior to his store opening he ran a series of full-page advertisements illustrated by the country's leading graphic artists. It was considered "one of the most extensive advertising campaigns ever prosecuted in the British Isles," presented with "a lavishness never before dreamed of in Britain."[61]

Other British stores learned the need for advertising from Selfridge, and learned it well.[62] In 1929 Harrods launched a series of three advertisements that set a high standard for cleverness. After inviting several venerated writers to contribute advertisements for the store and receiving their letters of refusal, Harrods published the refusal letters, which attracted considerable attention. It was a brilliant coup given their literary quality, which came across as humorous when published as advertisements. Featuring letters from H. G. Wells, Arnold Bennett, and George Bernard Shaw, the ads were also published in the New York Times. Editorial commentary in both the Times and Time magazine zeroed in on Shaw's self-serving claim that to accept payment from a "commercial enterprise for using his influence to induce the public to

OPPOSITE Bergdorf Goodman advertisement in the upscale British Country Life magazine in the 1920s, an era when only silk, linen, and wool were considered appropriate fabrics for clothes of distinction.

ABOVE Illustration by August Hajduk for furs at Berlin's KaDeWe, 1907.

RIGHT Men's topcoats in a Karstadt advertisement of 1937, with copy reading "back on top again," presumably a reference to the Depression. The Karstadt chain had fully "Aryanized" several years earlier.

FAR RIGHT Advertisement adopted from a 19th-century print by Ipposai Kuniyasu for Japan's Matsuzakaya stores.

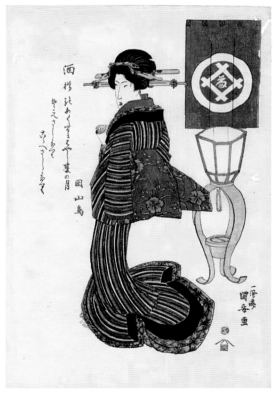

*An ensemble costume for town and
country, combining beige silk crepe
and kasha, trimmed in civet cat.
Imported by Bergdorf-Goodman.*

buy its wares" was a betrayal for a writer "who has been consecrated by Fame to the service of the public, and has thus become a prophet as well as an author."[63]

Moscow stores also produced some clever advertisements. One ad for GUM was the first commission for the Reklam-Konstruktor agency of Aleksandr Rodchenko and Vladimir Mayakovsky. The state-run department store, which had been using newspaper advertising since its opening in March 1922, needed eye-catching advertisements to compete with private retailers still in business.[64] Rodchenko and Mayakovsky's ad showed a "bourgeois" man juggling his possessions—bowler, bow tie, collar, pipe, watch, book by Pushkin, fountain pen, briefcase, Big Ben watch, and so on. The poster-sized advertisement filled a page in the July 1, 1923, Sunday edition of *Izvestia*.[65] Unlike most department stores, GUM aimed to fulfill men's needs quite as much as women's. Later Reklam-Konstruktor would come up with a slogan that captured the mission of Moscow's universal provider: "Clothe the body, Feed the stomach, Fill the mind—Everything that a person needs at GUM he will find."[66]

The 1920s marked the ascendancy of illustration in advertisements, especially as the number of pages in newspapers grew and it took more to attract a reader's attention.[67] Illustration was certainly not unknown before that decade—Selfridge hired prominent British artists for his 1909 blitz—but after the war, with the spread of modernism and fast-changing women's fashions, it increased in both quality and quantity. The artist began to take the lead away from the copywriter.[68]

It had long been an ambition of department-store owners to bring artists into their camp, although, like celebrated authors, well-known painters resisted kow-towing to commerce. After viewing William Powell Frith's painting *The Derby Day,* William Whiteley asked the artist if he would consider memorializing Whiteley's newly established store along the lines of the artist's *Westbourne Grove at 4 o'Clock in the Afternoon,* a scene that presumably would have included shoppers loaded with bundles. Frith declined the commission; nevertheless, the incident shows not only the value that artists represented to merchants but also the entrepreneurs' conviction that their activities could take on the mantle of high culture.[69] As the twentieth century progressed, many artists began to accept commissions for advertising work. In the 1920s and 1930s French department stores employed fashion illustrators such as Jean-Gabriel Domergue, Drian (Adrien Étienne), and René Vincent.[70] Domergue's advertising jobs did not prevent him from seeing his work in the Paris Salon in the 1920s or becoming a sought-after portrait painter.[71]

Because of their full-color capabilities, magazines offered department stores far better illustrative possibilities than newspapers for many decades. Although larger stores put out their own

ABOVE A sumptuous catalog cover illustrated by Drian (Adrien Étienne) for Printemps, 1910.

RIGHT Catalog cover for Galeries Lafayette by Jean-Gabriel Domergue, 1920.

fashion magazine-cum-catalog, Wanamaker may have been the only one to publish an independent magazine. He created *Everybody's Journal* in 1859, when he was only seventeen years old, publishing eighteen issues before its demise. He revived the magazine in 1899 and continued to publish it until 1903. Along with other advertising, it carried numerous full-page ads for the store.[72] Generally, however, unless a store had a customer base that extended far beyond its geographical domain, it made little sense to advertise in publications whose distribution was national or international. Some Paris stores such as the Grands Magasins du Louvre, a favorite with Americans, had enough business from tourists that they found it worthwhile to place ads in upscale magazines such as *Town & Country*.[73] Few other stores could take advantage of this medium, with the exception of Neiman Marcus, which began advertising in *Vogue* and *Harper's Bazaar* in the 1930s.[74] The Texas store was also able to capture business from American tourists passing through Dallas en route to Mexico.[75] In the 1940s more American stores, such as Macy's and Jordan Marsh, took out advertisements in magazines such as *Mademoiselle*, sometimes in partnership with name-brand dress manufacturers. Marshall Field, which had credit card customers throughout the country, ran advertisements in *Life*.[76]

Radio and, to a limited extent, television have been used to advertise department stores. For the purposes of selling radios when they had just been invented, some stores themselves obtained broadcasting licenses, erected aerials on their roofs, and aired programming such as live music, church services, and the reading of children's bedtime stories. Philadelphia department stores rapidly opened their own stations in 1922, whereas Boston stores came together to form a group station.[77] Selfridge wowed Londoners by broadcasting King George V's first radio speech in 1924 from loudspeakers outside the store, gathering a crowd that stopped traffic.[78] Rich's in Atlanta supplied programming that became part of the curricula of public schools in Atlanta and other Georgia towns.[79] Seibu began running TV commercials in the 1960s, an advertising method that works well for stores with branches spread regionally or nationally.[80] Many movies have used department stores as settings, but *Miracle on 34th Street* had an incalculable impact, not only because it was actually filmed in Macy's but also because Macy's used it as a springboard for an extensive promotional campaign.[81]

Department-store advertising became so important to newspapers over time that critics began to perceive that papers, which had formerly been mouthpieces for political parties, were becoming appendages of retailers.[82] This sounds like an exaggerated complaint, but department-store advertising dollars were certainly a major factor in keeping newspapers afloat. Loss of

Echoes of other children, other dreams

Three merry old toys that might delight an heir or join one's own lighthearted collection. In perfect working order, the Marklin copper steam engine from 1900. 16" high. $1,250. The Michel Marcu musical carousel, a reproduction in velvet spangled with glass prisms. 22" high. $300. The hand-made riding horse of hand carved wood, circa 1880, excellent condition. 33" long. 29" high. $300. From the turn of the century amusements on the frivolous Fourth Floor. At Field's in Chicago. There's nothing like it back home.

Marshall Field & Company

"Flowers 'B in your...

1 red,
4. The
Taylor

little fur jacket for au-
ith hand-stitched edges,
, $29.95. Saks-5th Ave.

undamental dress yet—thin
Perfect foil for your mass
r your little fur jacket, $29.9

This spring you'll wear a bang of flowers. This spring your hat looks straight-ahead. This spring your hat has an upward curve.

8.50

This spring your hat has a backward tilt. This spring your hat lifts your spirits high. Third Floor.

Lexington at 59th New York City

*B

LEFT A Bloomingdale's advertisement that appeared in a 1941 fashion magazine.

store ads could be a devastating blow, as happened when one million lines of advertising were lost with the closure of six big stores below 23rd Street in New York City in the 1910s. This meant not only the direct loss of revenue but also the loss of readers, as was vividly demonstrated when Wanamaker took his business away from a Philadelphia newspaper and its circulation immediately dropped by twenty thousand.[83] The sheer volume of department-store advertising was staggering. One year in the 1920s Lit Brothers of Philadelphia, for instance, took twenty-four full pages in the Sunday edition of a single newspaper to announce an anniversary sale.[84] In 1967 the director of Halle's said his store spent $2.3 million advertising in two newspapers, part of the $10 million spent yearly by Cleveland department stores.[85]

It has been claimed that newspapers occasionally suppressed news under pressure from a store. Selfridge, for example, did not like his store mentioned in stories about shoplifters being arrested.[86] Proof that newspapers' interests overlapped with stores' is demonstrated in the success of an association of Ohio retail merchants to persuade the secretary of the Ohio Newspaper Association to join them in lobbying President Franklin Roosevelt to change the date of Thanksgiving Day. It was scheduled to occur on the last Thursday of November, and that year, 1939, it would have fallen on the last day of the month. Roosevelt issued a proclamation that moved it up a week, and in 1941 Congress formally made the fourth Thursday, rather than the last, the official holiday. Thus the holiday cannot occur later than November 27, ensuring that the American holiday shopping season, which begins the day after Thanksgiving, will never begin fewer than twenty-seven days before Christmas.[87]

It had never been the intention of department stores to appear powerful. On the contrary, they wanted to be seen as progressive servants of modern commerce standing for honesty and affordable abundance. Consequently, they directed their advertising and public relations campaigns toward forging a store myth and personality. In most parts of the world department stores faced heavy opposition from small merchants in the economic downturn of the 1890s. Eaton's was not the only store that countered criticism by "creat[ing] the myth of itself," which extolled its innovative selling policies and progressive role in the community.[88] This approach, known as institutional advertising, sold the reputation of the store rather than specific merchandise.[89] An example is furnished by a 1944 Eaton's advertisement that, under the heading "Canada and Eaton's Have Grown Up Together," reported on how many store employees were in military service. The ad copy concluded with the stirring sentence, "Serving through peace and wars, through prosperity and depressions, Eaton's greets the war-scarred future with a sense of high opportunity and mighty

RIGHT Marshall Field's style magazine promotes travel to Mexico in 1932. American stores would return to Mexican-inspired styles and themes during World War II, when access to Europe was cut off.

responsibility."[90] A store's attempts to build its reputation could only go so far, however, if it violated propriety in a major way, as Printemps' director Jules Jaluzot did when he took depositors' money from his store's savings bank to pay for speculations in sugar futures, bankrupting the bank and wiping out the hard-earned nest eggs of employees and customers. In this case the store's slogan, *E Probitate Decus* (Honesty is my strength), was turned into a cruel joke.[91]

The concept of store personality was developed by John Wanamaker, the pioneer in so many aspects of promotion. By including a short homily in each full-page advertisement, accompanied by a facsimile of his striking signature, he signaled that he was guiding every move the store made. By this simple device, as someone noted in 1915, he gave "customers a sense of personal touch that they could not possibly have or feel, say, toward the Incorporated Dry Goods Company."[92] Harry Selfridge did something similar, producing newspaper columns from 1912 to 1939 under the pen name "Callisthenes" in which he discussed subjects ranging from retailing principles to the pleasures of shopping.[93] As it prepared to open a store in New York City, Gimbels hired a public relations firm to give the store a human dimension. Publicist George Perry ran stories in magazines about founder Adam Gimbel and his sons that left the impression of them as "hard-working boys who learned their business from sweeping floors up and who were taught truth and honor, and have become great and powerful." Perry believed that the portrait of the Gimbels created unconscious associations that would make all future advertising by the store more effective. He contrasted the Gimbel campaign with the "ponderous dignity" of the introductory advertising program conducted by another newly opened store, probably B. Altman. In this case, he felt, "Anything like a touch of color or human interest or democratic spirit was avoided like a pest," and the result was to leave the public cold.[94] Public relations also entailed making news, which department stores did almost effortlessly. Lectures on child care by psychologists; visits from film stars, best-selling authors, and fashion designers; and even spring openings and sewing contests for teenagers—all were newsworthy. Many newspapers routinely devoted a full page to department-store doings.[95] Stanley Marcus found the Dallas media eagerly awaiting his news. "In my efforts to meet their demands, I would find myself concocting a way-out imaginary tale about a man who had bought seven mink coats for his wife and six daughters, and a sable coat for his mistress," he recalled.[96] The media gobbled it up and he realized, "If we created one or more exotic gifts and put them in the catalogue, we would pick up coverage." Future catalogs featured "his and her" airplanes, a miniature submarine for two, and twin parasails.[97] Canadian and Australian stores won extensive coverage for royal visits, as did Mitsukoshi when Princess Diana visited in 1986 to preside over a sale of British goods.[98]

Window Gazing

Shop window displays are a sign of modernity that can still be read today as an indicator of how much a city has progressed beyond traditional retailing in outdoor market stalls.[1] From time immemorial, customers have patronized markets where, after careful hands-on examination of the goods, they enter into negotiation with the seller to determine how much they will pay. Window displays, in contrast, sell by tantalizing the imagination. The glass separating the viewer from the merchandise confers a sense of mystery on those objects.[2] The freedom with which the shopper can gaze upon objects of interest in display windows facilitates deliberation and comparison shopping. The seller enjoys an opportunity to present goods in the best possible light, while the shopper, freed from the seller's scrutiny, is permitted unlimited time to inspect the merchandise without interference or obligation. In the nineteenth century windows created a sensation for shoppers unaccustomed to seeing goods profusely displayed before their eyes. As the German historian Uwe Spiekermann has observed, "When gazing into the shop window, even a person with little income believed that the world was at his feet." It was this sense, real or imagined, that gave the display window its early fascination.[3]

Show windows, long a hallmark of the department store, have also served as beacons of civilization. A letter to the editor of the London *Times* gives a sense of how dark and gloomy a nighttime cityscape can be without the light and visual entertainment provided by show windows. Because London merchants of the 1890s shuttered their storefronts at night, anyone strolling about the streets had nothing to look at but blank facades. "London might," wrote a reader, "be made more like a city of the living than of the dead, by the simple device of bolting and barring the doors and leaving the windows of shops with their weekly display for the gaze of passers-by."[4] During wartime, window displays became symbols of normalcy and cheer. Even though they had little merchandise to show, Parisian stores remained dedicated to dispelling bleakness by keeping their windows colorful and attractive throughout World War II.[5]

Indeed, it was electric light that had the greatest impact on show windows. Because a disproportionate number of department stores have historically been located in the Northern hemisphere, doing their biggest business in the winter, darkness has always been their enemy. Lighted windows made a profound difference to the attractiveness of displays. From the dark streets, illuminated windows took on the look of theatrical stages—part real world, part dream world.[6]

Department-store window displays are a fundamental form of advertising. By the 1890s it was clear that retailing could not do without them. Until suburban shopping malls dispersed

ABOVE Although their size is undoubtedly exaggerated in this 1881 image of the windows surrounding the rue de Marengo entrance of the Grands Magasins du Louvre, their power to attract attention, especially when illuminated, is clear.

LEFT Spectators appear mesmerized by an Eaton's Queen Street Christmas window in 1955.

downtown crowds, easily a hundred thousand people a day could pass by a storefront in big cities. Seven thousand five hundred people per hour were counted passing along a busy block on Chicago's State Street in 1890—the block that would later be occupied by Carson Pirie Scott.[7] In the late 1940s, when department stores calculated sales figures for goods displayed in windows, analysts in the United States concluded that windows were directly responsible on average for one-third of sales.[8]

Window dressing was originally relegated to salesclerks with a degree of artistic talent who were able to wield a hammer and saw, but by the end of the nineteenth century it was a recognized profession. In the United States, professionalization was advanced by L. Frank Baum, who in 1898 founded the National Association of Window Trimmers. In 1900, just a few years before his *Wonderful Wizard of Oz* came out, Baum published *The Art of Decorating Dry Goods Windows and Interiors*. By 1895 Germany had more than a hundred companies that supplied racks, mannequins, and other props for showing merchandise in windows.[9] In Germany, France, and the United States, commercial art schools were teaching window decorating by the late 1890s.[10] About 1904 Tokyo's Mitsukoshi store, in preparation for its transition from an old-fashioned dry goods emporium to a modern department store, added windows to its storefront and sent two employees to an American window-dressing school in New York.[11] Many stores began to build up large window-dressing departments. Selfridges, for example, became London's first store to employ a large staff dedicated to window decorating and interior display when it opened in 1909.[12]

The professional approach, as articulated by Baum, emphasized that it was not enough merely to show the merchandise attractively; a successful window also had to capture the viewer's imagination. For this, art was needed. Around 1908 artists such as Elisabeth von Stephani-Hahn brought a new sensibility to the windows of Wertheim in Berlin.[13] Early show windows had been crammed with as much merchandise as possible, but people were beginning to realize that this approach was not effective because it made the goods on display appear cheap. French designers who read H. Glévéo's *Les Méthodes commerciales modernes*, published in 1923, learned that a single object, if spotlighted and framed, takes on an aura, a lesson shared with Dadaists, who selected ordinary objects to confer meaning on them in this way, if for different purposes.[14] The first real show windows that were both sizable and artistically decorated were created for Parisian stores. In the 1870s the Bon Marché had windows of "mighty plate-glass" that were "crowded with showy articles" of "delicate materials and more tints than . . . the rainbow."[15] France was famed for its Saint-Gobain glassworks, which set the world standard for quality and

PRECEDING PAGES At a time when window gazing was considered somewhat gauche, the fashion windows of Marshall Field in Chicago were nevertheless able to stop quite a few passersby, ca. 1910.

OPPOSITE Printemps mannequins of 1924 are so lifelike that they could be part of a living tableau, a form of display that did sometimes occur in department-store windows.

BELOW Both Gimbels and John Wanamaker had display windows at subway stops near their Philadelphia stores. This image is believed to be of Wanamaker's windows.

BOTTOM Fashion window at Selfridges in 1920.

production of polished plate glass. At the Paris Exposition of 1878 Saint-Gobain exhibited a magnificent piece of plate glass somewhat in excess of 21 by 13 feet (6.4 by 4 meters).

The rest of the world at this time did not have France's glass-making ability, but there were other barriers as well. A. T. Stewart's store on Ladies Mile in New York had many windows punctuating its cast-iron facade, but they were not large and displayed no goods.[16] This was by design, as Stewart felt that show windows were both unnecessary and undignified.[17] His conservatism was not unusual. It was based on the belief that if a merchant operated fairly and sold high-quality merchandise, a good reputation alone would sustain the business. Many felt that showy displays, like advertising, were an attempt to compensate for a poor reputation. Wealthy customers, in particular, preferred businesses that kept a low profile. Stewart's, for instance, even lacked an identifying sign. The London stores that catered to the aristocratic market upheld this tradition, as did, early on, Arnold Constable and John Daniell's in New York City, and Maison Gagelin in Paris.[18] Writing much later, designer Frederick Kiesler observed that "shops of reputation" patronized by the wealthy take on a club-like appearance, restricting their window display "to some permanent background of no special design, and showing only a few typical pieces of merchandise."[19]

Nonetheless, this conservative attitude was not conducive to transforming department stores into mighty businesses, and little by little it was overturned. In 1881 Simpson's in Toronto was still small but had two show windows flanking the door. By 1906 it had expanded and had 543 feet (165.5 meters) of windows.[20] Marshall Field's display windows also numbered only two in the 1880s but in 1890 it added several, and its Annex building, which opened in 1893, was outfitted with large modern show windows.[21] The twentieth century saw the institutionalization of the art of window dressing, as well as the spread of plate-glass production and improvements in window lighting. By 1915, half the world's supply of plate glass was being used in America, an amount that would double in the next ten years.[22]

The public actually had to learn to look into windows, an activity that was initially considered vulgar by the well bred. As late as the 1890s, anyone who would give windows more than a brief passing glance was regarded as either poor or an unsophisticated country bumpkin.[23] The anonymous journalist who called himself "the Spectator" struck a somewhat defensive tone in 1898 when he confessed that he numbered himself and the "president of one of the richest and most powerful banks in New York" among those who had the window-gazing habit. Exploiting social insecurities, department stores with lesser reputations hired well-dressed women who

ABOVE Entrance arcade at
Galeries Lafayette, ca.
1910. The rounded vitrines
resemble showcases and
break the monotony of the
flat facade.

OPPOSITE The window
display workshop in a
Karstadt store gives the
appearance of a
mannequin museum
spanning decades.

appeared to be upper class—but undoubtedly were not—to gaze raptly into their windows as a lure to get others to do the same.[24]

Britain was slower to accept show windows. Harry Gordon Selfridge may have exaggerated when he asserted that London stores had not learned how to dress windows in 1909 when he opened Selfridges. After all, Harrods boasted 1,890 running feet (576 meters) of ground-level windows in 1904. Yet there's little doubt that his methods did make quite an impression, particularly the habit of lighting windows at night rather than shuttering them, as was the custom.[25] Nevertheless, acceptance of show windows didn't come easily in London. Policemen revealed a deep-seated prejudice against them in 1910 when they began ticketing stores whose windows drew a crowd on the sidewalk. In response, merchants met with the police commissioner, arguing that having attractive windows was an achievement and asking that they be assigned a police officer to keep order, as was the custom with theater crowds. Their request was turned down with the retort that every establishment would like to have an officer outside because he would be a "walking advertisement."[26] Even in the United States, where the culture was more commercialized than Britain's in the early twentieth century, there was enough public discomfort with window displays that well into the century some stores, such as Marshall Field, Joseph Horne, and Dayton's, kept their windows shrouded on Sundays, and in some towns stores were required by ordinance to do so when "nude" mannequins were being dressed.[27]

Many factors affected the development of window design, including a growing middle class, which industrial workers aspired to join. As class ambitions rose, even the stores that specialized in bargains found that they had to appeal to those ambitions in order to sell goods. Consumers quickly learned to interpret window-display codes; windows crammed with goods, for instance, signaled that a store was not first class. In one fascinating case, a department store acquired a large job lot of imitation cut glassware and filled a show window with hundreds of pieces, attaching a large price card to each. To the management's surprise, the glassware did not sell despite the low prices. The store called in a troubleshooter, who removed most of the stock from the window, lined the display floor and backdrop with black velvet, selected a few pieces of glassware, placed them on pedestals, reduced the size of the price cards, and added several tall vases filled with American Beauty roses. The glassware then sold rapidly. The changes countered the impression that the glass was "common and cheap," treating it instead as though it were genuine cut glass. The elite presentation accorded with shoppers' notion that cut glass, even if imitation, represented luxury.[28]

The rise of ready-made fashion about 1910, as well as increasing fashion consciousness on the part of the public and the rapid turnover of styles, demanded a higher level of window art than dry goods and housewares had. Emphasis shifted from the steak to the "sizzle." Lifelike wax mannequins were introduced at this time, replacing the simple stands and headless, limbless dress forms used earlier.[29] The more realistic mannequins made it possible to create theatrical scenes. Coming from Paris firms such as Siégel & Stockman and Pierre Imans, which led the world in mannequin design, the figures had articulated limbs that could be arranged in lifelike positions.[30] Fashion display also encouraged stores to cut back on the mechanical special effects that had prevailed around the turn of the century because they distracted the viewer's gaze from the clothes. The man or woman staring at a rotating windmill or a ship rocking on a violent sea, for instance, tended not to notice hemlines or the cut of a jacket's lapels. The old rule of thumb that a crowd assembled on the sidewalk proved a window was successful, even if the object of people's attention was a mechanical panorama, gave way to greater focus on merchandise. Mechanical windows became stigmatized as cheap, suitable only for Christmas windows for children.[31]

Modernism influenced window display first in France and Germany before World War I, but it was slower to take hold in the United States and England. Berlin storekeepers participated in annual window-decorating competitions beginning in 1909, and some would claim that the city had the most advanced window design after 1923. Avant-garde abstract art, Bauhaus rationalism, Expressionist film, and the cult of pure machine style all inspired innovations in display.[32] Not until the late 1920s, several years after the 1925 Paris exposition of decorative arts, did American department stores embrace modern elements for window displays. Gradually, the old ways—seasonal themes in painted backdrops of seashores, snow, or autumn leaves, and latticework entwined with smilax—began to give way to zigzags and stark white plinths arrayed like skyscraper skylines. More daring stores, such as Saks Fifth Avenue in New York and Capwell in Oakland, California, adopted the streamlined mannequins with slit eyes, tiny mouths, and pointed chins and noses that had been introduced at the Paris exposition by Siégel & Stockman.[33] Yet, pragmatic doubts about "art" remained in some quarters throughout the 1920s. At a 1929 style conference, the chairman of Boston's Jordan Marsh voiced uncertainty about the selling power of modern art. "What we are all anxious to know," he remarked, "is whether the featuring of the element of Art [as represented by] the better design of merchandise, window displays and advertising has paid." Even though the Art Deco style

OPPOSITE An example of one of the more conservatively realistic Depression-era mannequins of the 1930s by Mannequins Siégel Paris, which replaced the more abstract figures of a few years earlier.

BELOW Comical expression on a Pierre Imans mannequin, ca. 1930.

was adopted for windows in department stores in New York, San Francisco, Boston, St. Louis, and even Davenport, Iowa, it was considered "dangerous" by some store managers because, like mechanical contraptions, it could overpower the merchandise.[34] Another fear was that modern windows, though eye-catching, might alienate customers who expected department stores to be dignified.

In the 1920s and 1930s a number of industrial designers in the U.S., including Norman Bel Geddes, Frederick Kiesler, and Raymond Loewy, would try their hand at window display, as would some fine artists, simply because it meant that more people would see their work than might view it in a museum. Among the artists who designed department-store windows or displayed their work in them at various times were Willem de Kooning in Utrecht, Georgia O'Keeffe in New York and Chicago, Andy Warhol in Pittsburgh and New York, Alexander Archipenko in New York, and Friedrich Vordemberge in Amsterdam.[35] The public was wary and more than ready to lodge protests, which often led to alterations or disassembly of displays. In 1939 Salvador Dalí grew angry at changes that Bonwit Teller made, in response to public complaints, to his surrealist tableau of a woman in a bathtub. In trying to restore his design he deliberately, or possibly accidentally, pushed the tub through the plate-glass window, making front-page news.[36] After receiving complaints, Bamberger's asked Marcel Duchamp to remove his nude-descending-a-staircase window in the Newark department store a mere two days after the window was unveiled in 1960.[37]

Display techniques were also borrowed from the theater. Windows had always been inspired by innovations in set design and lighting, but not until fashion became a dominant aspect of merchandising did window designers conceive of staging scenes full of human drama rather than simply lining up mannequins in stiff ensembles. The dramatic possibilities of mannequins had been hinted at when Stockman Brothers created a scenario depicting a struggle at a fair-grounds stand in their presentation of mannequins at the 1900 Exposition Universelle in Paris.[38] In the early 1920s Parisian store windows featured scenes such as Red Cross workers and children playing games at a party.[39] The Surrealist movement brought mystery to tableaux, as exemplified by a Saks window in New York in which Marcel Vertes presented a mannequin reclining on a psychoanalyst's couch, sublimating her desires with visions of a new frock.[40]

Theatrical influences increased in the 1930s as unemployed stage designers came looking for jobs in window design.[41] A Lord & Taylor window depicting a jitterbugging sailor on the upper level while an elderly couple below banged on their ceiling with a broomstick exemplified the

ABOVE The radically modern look of mannequins of the late 1920s, on display at de Bijenkorf in Rotterdam.

Triumph Die Krönung der Figur

Wir wünschen
unseren Kunden
ein segensreiches
1958

LEFT One of a series of surrealistic windows at Bergdorf Goodman in January 1938.

OPPOSITE Built in 1928 as seven separate store-fronts, the now unified Bergdorf Goodman has a choice location on Fifth Avenue overlooking Central Park, and its display windows attract a great deal of attention.

"theater of social occasion," as it was dubbed during World War II.[42] Actress Rosalind Russell, in person, vamped in a Bonwit Teller window, tearing away at wrapping paper covering the panes, dressed in a negligee and mimicking a similarly dressed mannequin created by display director Gene Moore, a master of theatricality.[43] In Tokyo, a department store featured not only brides and bridal parties, a mainstay of department-store windows, but also a sophisticated, well-dressed businessman with his cocktail table and magazine rack displaying the *New York Times*.[44] It wasn't until the 1970s, however, that theatrical department-store windows became entertainment venues, once again provoking the question, "Does it sell merchandise?" It certainly helped raise Bloomingdale's profile when Candy Pratts masterminded windows in which "happenings" were staged with languorous nudes, murder victims, groups of women in sexually ambiguous scenarios, and kitchen mishaps in process—scenes often accompanied by smashed objects ranging from eggs to Christmas ornaments. To achieve the right poses, Pratts's staff often had to disassemble mannequins and staple them back together. Only New York and a few other cities would tolerate windows of this sort. In Chicago, the display manager at Carson Pirie Scott said he appreciated humor, and had himself gone so far as to deploy several windows to depict a woman's preparations for the evening, her visits to bars and parties, and her return home, where she collapsed with an icebag to her head. But the chairman of Sanger-Harris in Dallas was bluntly negative, saying: "Those windows up there [i.e., New York City] are dressed to attract the same kind of strange people who pass by on the sidewalk there."[45] At the time Pratts was directing Bloomingdale's display department, Bob Currie entertained window gazers at Bendel's in New York with similar scenes. What's fascinating about Pratts's and Currie's depiction of unhealthy and dead subjects is how they accentuated the corpselike appearance of mannequins, a characteristic that had long been recognized by the display trade. Curiously, by emphasizing the mannequins' stillness, they succeeded in bringing scenes alive in a way that neither animated windows nor the customary decorous posing of mannequins had been able to do.

When British-born Simon Doonan came to New York City's Barneys in the mid-1980s, he pushed the irreverent style of window decorating a step further, extending it into the semisacred realm of Christmas. The upscale specialty store, which had been founded by Barney Pressman in 1923 as a bargain-priced men's clothing store, had grown into a fashionable retailer also carrying women's clothing, as well as select housewares and gift items. But it was still operating in its original location at Seventh Avenue and 17th Street, well outside the ambit of

BELOW A red-tinted window display of handbags at Bloomingdale's during the 2008 Christmas season brims with holiday excess.

OPPOSITE *Saturday Night Live*'s Coneheads celebrate Christmas 2009 in a Barneys New York window under the direction of designer Simon Doonan.

Two recent holiday
windows at Bergdorf
Goodman: boxing polar
bears (left) and an Alice in
Wonderland–inspired
window by the store's
David Hoey (above).

OPPOSITE Recent Selfridges windows evoking a 1960s American roadtrip.

ABOVE A Barneys window promoting a line of men's suits, 2009.

RIGHT The Dior window in a Printemps display celebrating the History of Elegance, May–June 2010. Each window featured a luxury brand, represented by its iconic product and rendered in the store's symbolic colors.

tourists and other visitors to the city whose business counts heavily for holiday sales. The wicked humor displayed in the windows created by Doonan and his crew was a cure for that, successfully transforming the store into a prime destination for holiday shoppers from out of town. These were decidedly not Christmas windows for children.[46]

The windows, which are known for their excessive and deliberate "bad taste," have lampooned celebrities, political figures, and other luminaries such as Vice President Dan Quayle, Prime Minister Margaret Thatcher, and Madonna—or whoever figured largely, better yet foolishly, in the news of any given year. Occasionally a window has offended public taste, as happened with a "Hello Kitty" nativity scene by artist Tom Sachs in 1994 that portrayed the Madonna and Christ Child in the guise of the popular toy figures, showing the "Virgin Mary" kitty dressed in leather with her legs splayed.[47] In 1993 Barneys opened a new store at Madison and 61st Street that carried on the holiday-window tradition of the original store, which was closed in 1997. Barneys' windows illustrate that the art of window decoration, introduced by department stores more than a century ago, has not lost its relevance or magnetic popular appeal.

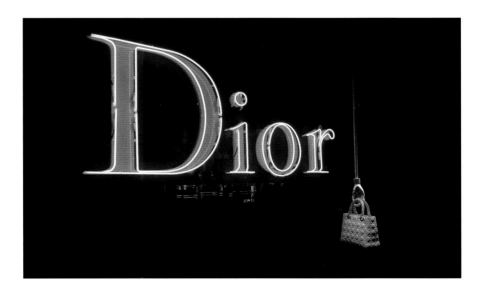

Merchandising Spectacles

One of the biggest, most fundamental revolutions brought about by department stores had less to do with *how* they displayed merchandise than with the fact *that* they displayed it. In contrast to the old-style dry goods stores, which often had signs advising shoppers to ask for merchandise they did not see, department stores insured that goods would no longer be "stacked in out-of-the-way corners accessible only through the intermediary of a salesclerk, but placed where they could be touched and arranged so as to play on the consumer's senses."[1] Interior displays went several steps beyond window displays, which tantalized only the sense of sight; once the shopper entered the store she could handle the goods, and in many cases smell and taste them as well. Display changed the experience of shopping. Whereas once upon a time shopping consisted of acquiring a list of items drawn up in advance, it now frequently meant impulse buying. After World War II most people entering a department store would buy something on a whim, mainly because they had seen it on display.[2]

Display meant that clerks had a lesser role in selling. In the words of a manager at the Emporium in San Francisco, "The goods sell themselves, and the clerks merely wrap them up and take the money."[3] The term *visual merchandising* was coined in recognition of the importance of display, wrought initially by the replacement of solid-wood storage cabinets with glass cases. The actual term came into use when self-service was introduced during the labor shortages of World War II, but the concept was fundamental to modern department-store selling from the start. Shoppers were meant to be so entranced by what they saw that they felt compelled to buy it.

Among the most striking features of nineteenth-century French stores were their displays. "The moment you enter the building by one of the great doors, you are dazzled with the display of riches,—curtains, Oriental carpets, lace hung on the walls, piles of linen, of silk, of satins, of plush, of velvet, flung on the counters, robes and mantles displayed, cart-loads of gloves, rich furniture, costly *bibelots* . . ." noted a journalist summing up the visual impact of Paris department stores in 1884.[4] Rugs, shawls, and silk fabrics were hung from the banisters of upper galleries. Counters, walls, and pillars were put into service as display fixtures, with bolts of fabrics draped in cascades from pillars starting at least 10 feet (3 meters) from the floor.[5] Asian merchandise such as lanterns, screens, vases, baskets, fans, and umbrellas from China and Japan was given prominent display space. Umbrellas and fans, probably the most splashily colorful goods on the market in the nineteenth century, were shown opened and massed in stunning arrays, while vases and baskets were often grouped along the edges of staircases.[6]

PRECEDING PAGES
LEFT Mannequins silhouetted against windows in Galeries Lafayette.
RIGHT A child-size green leather armchair holds toy bears from Harrods.

BELOW Artist's depiction of fabrics in the Hall Marengo of the Grands Magasins du Louvre, ca. 1910.

RIGHT Painting of the busy main floor at the Leonhard Tietz store in Düsseldorf, 1920. No old-style partitions or tall cabinetry obstruct the view.

PRECEDING PAGES
Handkerchief department
at Harrods, ca. 1920.
Assisting customers with
this merchandise could be
time consuming.

OPPOSITE Mannequins
pose inside a large
circular vitrine at
Printemps in the 1920s.
The case has the
advantage of both
presenting an ensemble
and preventing customers
access.

ABOVE Women's
foundation garments on
the main floor of
Printemps, ca. 1920.
Clearly this was a
department designed in
recognition that
customers need help in
finding a girdle that fits
properly.

Another important feature of French department stores that enhanced display was their open-ness. The full effect of the merchandise relied upon open floorplans as well as the daylight from glass ceilings. Unlike the old dry goods stores, French department stores did not partition off departments from one another. Shoppers entering the building immediately grasped a store's expanse, its layout, and the wealth of merchandise it contained. The French way of or-ganizing space, in sharp contrast to the darkness and hidden merchandise of the traditional small shop, would become the norm throughout the world by the turn of the century. Even though some stores in other parts of the world did not have atriums, all but the most conser-vative stores adopted plans that maximized openness and good lighting. Ceilings on a store's ground floor were always several feet higher than on upper floors, and mezzanines with deco-rative railings imparted a feeling of greater spaciousness to stores that lacked atriums.

In the 1890s and the early twentieth century, department-store business grew so fast that many stores could not keep up with expanded departments and the proliferation of merchandise. A careful examination of early-twentieth-century postcards and advertising images of store inte-riors reveals that they coped by squeezing merchandise tables and display cases into the niches between pillars and along gallery railings overlooking atriums.[7] Every bit of the store's architecture became a prop and a background for goods. Square pillars, fashioned by boxing in the slender steel support posts, were fitted with glass shelving on all four sides. Merchandise was often stacked up on the floor around pillars as well.[8] Metal stands, shelving units, and rows of suspended rods sat on counters and ran overhead, holding gloves, handkerchiefs, ar-tificial flowers, and other small items. A bower effect was created by arching rods holding more merchandise over aisles. Product displays and large cardboard advertising pieces hovered on ledges and cabinet tops. Ground floors, which, as seen in lithographed images of early stores, had once been spacious, almost empty looking, became packed with tables and counters, nar-rowing aisles to the point that traffic was almost immobilized.

The construction of additions and new store buildings alleviated crowding, for a time at least. The ideal became one of orderly profusion. Merchants learned more about the psychology and physiology of display, repositioning merchandise displays inside the shoppers' "belt of vision," a zone that began 2 feet (0.6 meters) from the floor and went up to about 7 feet (2.1 meters).[9] To position merchandise within the belt of vision, it was lifted up from the floor onto tables and counters, and rugs and fabrics were removed from upper-floor banisters, perhaps also to conform with more stringent fire regulations. Displays once considered a model, such as those

found in the fancy goods department of the Charles Jenner store in Edinburgh in 1895, where tables were overflowing with merchandise and Japanese screens and baskets were heaped on the floor, would no longer pass muster in the twentieth century.[10]

The modern changeover from solid-wood cabinetry to glass cases and counters facilitated the shopper's view of merchandise without strewing things across every surface. It also provided a way to enhance the value of goods. The simple act of placing a handbag or a pair of gloves inside a glass case suggested that the objects were too valuable to be left in the open at the mercy of shoplifters or dirty fingers. Like the show windows outside the department store, merchandise in cases tantalized viewers by being so close yet out of reach. John Wanamaker, who was critical of display methods used by nineteenth-century museums because he felt they jumbled objects together, was quick to borrow the idea of showing merchandise in glass cases after he saw them in Paris.[11] Elimination of partitions and tall cabinets gave the department store a more modern, horizontal appearance. In London, however, some of these changes did not take place until after the arrival of Selfridge, who brought American methods to London when he opened in 1909. Then, suddenly, in many stores, "the long rows of mahogany counters were ripped out and the main floors converted into salons with nicely decked glass cases."[12]

And yet there was such a thing as too much order in the presentation of goods. At their artful best, department-store displays balanced luxury and orderliness with messy profusion. In many ways the success of the entire department-store industry came from blending high and low cultural forms, the hushed reverence of the cathedral with the gasps and cheers of crowds applauding circus acts. Going too far in either direction could hurt a business whose goal was to market goods as broadly as possible. Presenting hats and gloves primly arranged in glass cases ran the risk of looking austere and stingy. Messiness could be perilous, yet there was something about heaps of merchandise being mauled by jostling shoppers that engaged more elemental passions and drew onlookers into the fray. As one scholar has theorized, an excess of goods suggested that objects were inexhaustible, which was deeply meaningful to shoppers who had once known want and scarcity.[13]

The spectacle of thousands of massed objects, even if they were all identical bars of soap, had its own majesty and, further, suggested that the store did a tremendous volume of business. This was nowhere more evident than at Paris white sales, *expositions de blancs*, despite the fact that much of the merchandise comprised nothing more exciting than folded bundles of sheets and pillowcases. The stores handled the goods cleverly, using them as building blocks to re-create

PRECEDING PAGES
Accessories departments at Printemps, located on the main floor under the dome, ca. 1920, were expected to produce the highest returns per square foot. Although the main-floor counters have plenty of space around them, on the store's upper floors merchandise is pushed up against the galleries' decorative railing, creating a messy appearance.

ABOVE French perfume department in the new John Wanamaker store, Philadelphia, ca. 1911.

FAR LEFT Interior of the Galeries Lafayette branch established in London in the 1920s.

LEFT The lace department is in the foreground of the grand atrium of Wertheim on Leipziger Strasse in Berlin, ca. 1910.

OPPOSITE The grand atrium hall of Leonhard Tietz in Cologne, 1920s, with mannequins dressed in costumes, probably for a celebration of Carnival.

LEFT Although fine foods and wines as offered in Harrods food hall add to the reputation of a department store, early department stores discovered that basic groceries do not. Given the popularity of these departments in stores today, it is surprising how virulently they were criticized around the turn of the last century.

spectacular examples of nearly full-size provincial buildings complete with shingles and lace-curtained windows.[14] At its 1926 white sale, the Tietz store on Leipziger Strasse in Berlin used white cloth to cover lanterns, casting a spectral light. Arched openings on upper-floor galleries surrounding the central lightwell sent out a glow from within white-covered cornices accented by a second arched tier of small white bulbs. At other times the store had created textile displays in the form of Indian temples, Roman victory arches, waterfalls, and ships docked at a pier.[15]

Harrods' food hall is a prime example of the almost overwhelming effect of staged abundance particularly evident in the Christmas season, when row after row of turkeys hung from the walls and ducks and geese were draped over marble tables as though presenting the triumphal bounty of a royal hunt (see pages 86–87). Rooms with crates and crates of eggs, rows of decorated cakes on pedestals tilted up toward the customers, pigs with front and back legs stretched out, piglets on their backs, and tables piled high with roasts and big slabs of bacon suggested that no one could ever go hungry in Britain, even during the Depression.[16] In the 1980s, however, a time when many venerable stores undertook historic restoration projects, Harrods cleared out salamis hanging from the meat hall ceiling to permit spectators to admire the Royal Doulton tiles of 1902 designed by ceramacist W. J. Neatby (see above, as well as on pages 86–87).

Display was relied upon to heighten the appeal of what was being sold in a variety of ways. The glamorous buildings so many department stores occupied helped alleviate the "problem" of making mass-produced goods seem luxurious. Elaborate architecture and fittings in the grand stores created a "jewel-box effect" that lifted even as mundane an item as muslin underwear to a higher plane.[17] Even when buying a corset cover or a black umbrella, the customer was taking home a bit of the store's glamour. It has been suggested that the container became more important than its contents, thus permitting the department store to sell the "idea of luxury" more than real luxury objects.[18] As evidence that "ordinary, everyday commodities, reflected in their opulent surroundings, became signs of wealth and affluence," consider the preference of Tokyo's consumers for department stores as sources of gift boxes of soap, for instance, to present to their bosses during the Japanese gift-giving season. Although presentation boxes of soap sold there were identical to those sold in small shops, they connoted a higher level of respect for the recipient simply because the former came from Mitsukoshi or Takashimaya or another big department store.[19]

The value-enhancing impact of display was also served by the tactic of presenting rare and expensive goods that were beyond the purse of most of the store's customers. Stores put the

ABOVE The food hall at Globus in Zurich.

OPPOSITE Fresh produce at the Bon Marché's food hall, La Grande Épicerie.

Opposite Men's casual clothes at Bloomingdale's in New York, 2009.

Top Confectionery department at Bergdorf Goodman, New York, 2009. Small and paneled, this self-contained chocolatier would be at home on a street in Paris.

Above Self-service packaged underwear at Bloomingdale's, New York, 2008.

Right Raincoats are displayed against specially painted panels that set them off, Galeries Lafayette, Paris, 2010.

real thing on display, but sold the copy. This did not involve deception—customers knew they were getting a product modeled on, but *not* a couture dress or a genuine diamond bracelet. Yet the presence of the real thing created the illusion that the store handled valuable merchandise and that there were indeed customers who bought it. Who was to know that deluxe merchandise often did not sell and ended up inside the closet of the store executive's family? The basic strategy was much the same as in museum shops today. After seeing Monet's *Water Lilies,* museum goers want to take home a little bit of its magic with them, even if it's only a decorated tee shirt or tote bag. Stores wishing to burnish their reputation for stylishness initiated what would become the museum-store approach. In 1928, for instance, Lord & Taylor mounted a decorative arts exhibit featuring furniture from the French exposition of 1925. The pieces were not for sale, further enhancing the value of modern design, which, the exhibit suggested, was of museum quality. Later the store would open its own department of modern furniture.[20]

Display was closely connected with store events such as festivals in which unusual merchandise from "exotic" places was put on sale in settings decorated with flowers, streamers, and caged birds during themed events that replicated Japanese apple blossom festivals, Parisian street fairs, or American carnivals (see page 97).[21] The origins of the merchandise were important, but no more than the festival air surrounding its presentation. Events featuring product demonstrations were another form of display that brought the merchandise to life by showing how it might be used by an idealized consumer. It took a determined display expert at Marshall Field's to convince executives that the store had to lighten up, change its displays frequently, and create activity with events such as cooking lessons by chefs in the kitchen equipment department, but once the value of such events was recognized there was no turning back.[22]

Although the basic principles of display have not changed fundamentally since the early days, they have evolved as the circumstances under which stores operate have necessitated. Department-store interiors today are sleeker and more open, more flexibly arranged, and have a greater number of displays. Gone are long rows of counters and wide main aisles straight as airplane runways. Flooring is used strategically to orient and direct shoppers and to unify and identify the store's "brand," which often must compete with branded merchandise occupying manufacturer-designed mini-shops in the store. Increasingly, mannequins are used on the sales floor in imaginative and often humorous interactive groupings. Apart from their entertainment value, the mannequins signal the store's interpretation of current fashion.[23]

Because of the need to refresh and resize departments frequently and to permit customers to serve themselves, one of department stores' classic, signature furnishings, the counter, has begun to disappear. Even cosmetic departments, once counter strongholds, have opened up, with products on shelving accessible to customers who can experiment with the merchandise and evaluate prices without pressure from salesclerks working on commission.

In recent years, as many department stores sought to enter the luxury market, they have taken cues from display strategies evolved by specialty stores, the best of which have perfected what might be called "the art of the container." For stores such as the new Barneys New York in Chicago, which salutes the architecture of Louis Sullivan's Carson Pirie Scott store, the container has become the entire building, with stunning design features such as a floating stairwell, dramatic geometric flooring, and decorative metal sculpture by John-Paul Philippé.

Department stores, occupying far more space than most luxury stores, are usually unable to commission new buildings and must work with the limitations of their existing physical plants. But, like smaller retailers, they have learned how to create excitement and enhance store identity via interior display techniques. Up against the dazzling, image-soaked presence of the Internet, stores must provide shoppers with a reason to leave home. In the words of veteran visual marketing and display expert Martin Pegler, "Shoppers, now more than ever, are looking for entertainment in the retail store and that entertainment is often to be found in displays."[24]

PRECEDING PAGES Fine jewelry, Bergdorf Goodman, New York, 2010. These ground-floor galleries look out on Fifth Avenue. The mirrored counters hide custom-designed safes.

TOP LEFT Barneys New York, Chicago branch, 2009.

BOTTOM LEFT Perfume department, Barneys New York, Chicago branch, 2009.

OPPOSITE Women's clothing displayed sparsely on the recently renovated third floor of Saks Fifth Avenue, New York City. Fewer items on display has long indicated better merchandise at higher price.

OVERLEAF Men's clothes are presented at Bergdorf Goodman's clubby men's store across Fifth Avenue from the main store, following a long-standing department-store tradition of separating men's and women's shopping areas.

BRIONI

大正六年六月一日發行

第七卷　第六號

Services and Circuses

The department store's concept of service encompasses a galaxy of activities. At its most basic level, of course, service entails waiting upon customers, presenting them with merchandise, providing information, and completing the sales transaction. But department stores have gone far, far beyond the basics. For the past 150 years or so, observers have tried to capture the full scope and meaning of department stores with words and phrases such as "more than a store," "institution," and "community center."[1] Because of the range and variety of events hosted by department stores, marketing professor Paul Nystrom of Columbia University declared in 1919, "The modern store is almost as much an amusement place as it is a merchandising establishment."[2]

Services and events are intended to attract shoppers and keep them from leaving the store, the underlying notion being that the longer they spend looking at merchandise, the more likely they are to buy. Historically, department stores have found it essential to engage in a process of "intensive cultivation" of both their customers and their expensive real estate.[3] Customer cultivation also extends to customers outside the store—those who live far away or whose needs require complex coordination of skilled craftspeople to produce a customized solution.

The early proto-department stores offered few amenities. Indeed, it was considered remarkable that A. T. Stewart's Astor Place store in 1862 offered "even such an elementary convenience as a toilet for women customers."[4] In 1890 big stores devoted perhaps 5 percent of their budgets to services, but it was estimated that about twenty-five years later they spent as much on services as they did on the merchandise they sold.[5] The reason for the proliferation of services was a simple one: competition. In the 1890s department stores were engaged in a fierce rivalry with one another; by the 1920s they faced new competition—from chain stores and women's specialty shops.

As they developed, stores fashioned themselves as urban destinations "that celebrated a notion of leisure built around consumption."[6] The culmination of this approach occurred in Japan in the latter half of the twentieth century. But Japanese entrepreneurs were building upon a long tradition derived from their own culture's traditional bazaars, as well as from earlier department stores in other parts of the world.[7] In Berlin in 1900, if a woman said, "We're going to Wertheim," it did not mean that she needed to buy anything in particular but was "talking about an excursion" that might involve an afternoon spent with an acquaintance strolling through the large stores, enjoying the surroundings, and stopping for a cup of tea in one of their restaurants. When it was time to go home, shoppers often realized that "instead of the bow tie, which one initially intended to buy, one is loaded down with a whole bundle of the most varied kinds of things."[8]

PRECEDING PAGES

LEFT In the first decades of the 20th century soda fountains were popular in department stores all over the world. Mitsukoshi had one by 1918, as demonstrated on the cover of the store's magazine, illustrated by Hisui Sugiura.
RIGHT Galeries Lafayette delivery truck, 1930.

BELOW Employees report for work at Abraham & Straus in Brooklyn, 1909. The photograph is by social reformer Lewis Hine, who documented evidence of child labor in the big stores.

OPPOSITE

Uniformed delivery staff in front of a loading dock at Printemps, Paris, ca. 1930.

Harry Gordon Selfridge theorized that people came to a big department store because it was "so much brighter than their homes," an observation likely to have been literally true before World War I, when many homes were without electricity.[9] By the early twentieth century it was considered essential to plan stores with a full array of amenities, as demonstrated by the prospectus of a store planned for Des Moines, Iowa, in 1906:

> A soda fountain, with luncheonettes will also be on the first floor. The top floor will contain dining and lunch rooms, similar in plan to Field's in Chicago. A palm garden will occupy the roof. A very original and delightful feature of the building will be a large auditorium where frequent entertainments will be given for the patrons of the store. It will be so arranged that art works may be exhibited. The store will thus be a center of music and art, not alone for Des Moines, but for the State of Iowa. Parlors and rest rooms, fitted up in metropolitan style, will occupy a space on the third floor. Complete hair dressing and manicuring rooms will be opened with first class attendants. Plans for the best dressmaking establishment west of New York are already perfected. A postoffice department is contemplated.[10]

French stores were the first to include areas designed solely to entertain and refresh shoppers. In the 1870s the Bon Marché furnished an oak-paneled reading room with a large reading table and high-back green velvet chairs. Journals and newspapers in French and English, stereoscopes for viewing images of Paris, and pens, ink, and writing paper were provided "free-gratis, for nothing."[11] The Paris store also contained a ladies' "retiring room" filled with flowers, plants, and a bubbling fountain—an arrangement that would be duplicated by Wertheim's grand turn-of-the-century store in Berlin, where the young artist George Grosz liked to take his girlfriend to tea.[12] In the 1890s Marshall Field equipped lounges and lavatories with talcum powder, hairpins, shoelaces, and sewing notions for emergency repairs in case a shopper's outfit fell into disarray.[13] Modeled after Marshall Field, Selfridges also provided minor dress repairs for free.[14] Tokyo's Mitsukoshi store served tea without charge to women in its restrooms and dedicated space for a club room for scholars and journalists.[15]

Lavatories and spacious, well-furnished lounges were two amenities that helped make department stores resemble women's clubs. As women comprised up to 85 percent of a department store's customers, management bent over backward to attract them to—and keep them on—the premises. They created feminine environments, beginning with architecture, as exemplified by the exterior and interior ornamental detail of Chicago's Schlesinger & Mayer store (later Carson Pirie Scott), which a critic described as expressively feminine.[16] Live music also marked stores as feminine at a time when music was perceived as a female domain. Women responded by using stores not just as shopping venues but as their social headquarters. At appointment registries and concierge desks inside the main doors, they left messages for friends who might be available later for lunch or tea. Little wonder that the women of Ardmore, Pennsylvania, called the Strawbridge & Clothier's branch that opened there in 1930 "the Ardmore Club."[17]

Restrooms and restaurants in the big stores dated to the 1890s, but most other services designed to please women were introduced in the early twentieth century, as stores expanded and became more luxurious. In 1907 Berlin's KaDeWe pioneered an in-store hairdressing salon, and the trend blossomed in the 1920s. With names such as the Temple of Venus or the Bobber Shop, in-store salons expressed women's new liberation from Victorian conventions. By mid-century, G. Fox in Hartford, Connecticut, boasted one of the largest beauty salons in the United States, employing a staff of forty-five. Charm classes were also introduced to instruct teen-age customers in hair styling, makeup, and poise.[18]

Custom dressmaking, bridal salons, and fashion shows added an element of glamour and helped attract more affluent shoppers who had disdained the big stores for their racks of undistinguished mass-produced clothing. Invariably, custom salons in stores outside of France were called Gray Salons (French gray being a fashionable color) or simply French Shops. The salons—consisting of small, carpeted, and mirrored rooms where a customer might view clothing modeled solely for her—proliferated in the early 1950s. Gimbels hired renowned designer Raymond Loewy to re-model its New York store in 1951, creating stylish salons for furs, evening wear, and bridal gowns.[19]

Fashion shows began to grow in popularity in the 1910s, about the time that it became sufficiently respectable for women to parade themselves in public. The Hermann Tietz store claimed to have put on the first department-store fashion show in Berlin, around 1911. Georg Tietz contacted fashion houses in Paris, among them Jeanne Lanvin, which collectively loaned him thirty cases of hats, shoes, dresses, and coats, as well as fifteen live models for a tour of the Hermann Tietz chain.[20] Tokyo's Mitsukoshi held its first fashion show in 1927, the year it installed air conditioning. In the 1950s many stores presented not only frequent, sometimes daily, fashion shows in their restaurants, but also annual charity fashion extravaganzas so large that they were held in hotels or city auditoriums. Shows presented by stores such as Marshall Field in Chicago, Eaton's and Simpson's in Toronto, and Rich's in Atlanta long enjoyed status as major social events.

ABOVE Fur salon in Oslo's Steen & Strøm, 1920. Salons, designed to win wealthier customers, were modeled on Paris, dressmaking establishments.

OPPOSITE A saleswoman attends to a customer in the millinery salon at Mexico City's Palacio de Hierro, 1920.

ABOVE A customer is fitted for a wedding gown at a Wanamaker store, 1953.

RIGHT A tailor helps a Nordiska Kompaniet customer with dress alterations, 1950.

TOP Sophie Gimbel, fashion director at Saks Fifth Avenue, makes last-minute adjustments on models.

ABOVE A technician gives a facial at NK, 1950.

PRECEDING PAGE
A stylish woman ponders
the latest fashions at a de
Bijenkorf store, 1952.

OPPOSITE The
"refreshment room" of the
Althoff store, Dortmund
(later Karstadt), with its
decorative painted ceiling,
1920s.

In Paris it was the custom to serve tea or other refreshments to clients as they sat in couturiers' salons viewing designs and being fitted with gowns. The Bon Marché and other stores borrowed the practice of pampering their customers from couturier Charles Frederick Worth. Next to the reading room in the Bon Marché was a buffet that offered cakes and biscuits, along with cups of hot chocolate or glasses of Madeira and claret served with "dainty finger napkins, brilliant glass," and filtered ice water.[22] London's "universal provider," William Whiteley, tried to import this service to his store in Bayswater in 1872, but Londoners were far less receptive than the French to women consuming alcoholic beverages, and the authorities rejected his license application. A newspaper snidely commented that "sherry and silks, or port and piqués, need not of necessity go together when ladies go 'shopping,'" and a popular journal designated his lunchroom a "dangerous" Paris import that in itself promoted "excessive shopping."[23]

No alcoholic beverages were served in United States or Canadian department-store restaurants either. Anti-department-store forces of the 1890s objected even to the sale of wines by the bottle in the stores.[24] The virtuous soda fountain dispensing non-alcoholic beverages and ice cream and the non-alcoholic tea room were thus almost synonymous with American department stores in the early twentieth century. Not until the opening of its custom design shop in 1941 did Marshall Field permit alcohol inside the store, and it did not enter the doors of Hudson's in Detroit until the opening of their art gallery in 1963.[25]

As America struggled with liquor issues, refreshment salons in French stores—which did serve wine—grew in popularity. An observer recorded that on busy days at the Bon Marché in 1884 the buffet turned into "a battle-field where the women and children fight for a drink of syrup."[26] German stores offered customers beer, but the American soda fountain also found favor in them. The Hermann Tietz store on Leipziger Strasse in Berlin installed a marble one with a hundred silver spigots in 1903.[27] Selfridges' soda fountain introduced Londoners to ice cream with high butterfat content, a new experience for a public used to Italian ice sold by street vendors.[28]

From refreshment salons and soda fountains, store food service grew into more complete lunchrooms and restaurants. The dry goods firm Shirokiya was the first in Japan to open an in-store restaurant, where it served sushi and noodles, in 1904. The restaurant was enlarged when the store was rebuilt in 1911.[29] About this time Mitsukoshi opened a dining room that was furnished with long tables seating up to a dozen diners each. In addition to local dishes, the restaurant served Western cakes and cream puffs.[30] And a soda fountain on the store's roof served ice cream.[31] In 1922 the Mitsukoshi restaurants, which now included a separate Western-style dining room,

ABOVE A three-tiered tea
tray at Harrods.

LEFT Lunch counter in
Zion's Cooperative
Mercantile Institution
(ZCMI) in Salt Lake City,
1937.

BELOW Soda fountain in
the Leonhard Tietz store,
Cologne, ca. 1920.

could accommodate nine hundred people at a time, and by 1933 the store was serving ten thousand meals a day during the week and many more on weekends and holidays.[32] In the mid-1970s the Mitsukoshi store in Nihonbashi contained no fewer than thirty-five restaurants offering cuisine from around the world.[33]

Although many American department-store restaurants were closed during the Depression or replaced with snack bars and lunch counters, some stores such as Rich's in Atlanta, Meier & Frank in Portland, Oregon, and Joseph Horne in Pittsburgh considered restaurants central to their appeal. In addition to serving as meeting places for the women of the city, store restaurants hosted daily fashion shows at noon and Santa Claus lunches for children during the Christmas holidays. How great an asset a large and stately store restaurant could be was demonstrated in 1954, when the David Jones store in Sydney held a state banquet for Queen Elizabeth in a flower-filled seventh-floor hall overlooking a "gaily illuminated Hyde Park."[34] In recent years many department-store restaurants in Europe have been refurbished, some as top-flight eating establishments, becoming major attractions in their own right.

Roof gardens were often turned into restaurants in the days before air conditioning became common. In the early twentieth century Printemps would place tables on its rooftop terrace every spring and summer so that lunchers and afternoon tea drinkers could enjoy a view of Paris.[35] Filene's in Boston had a rooftop restaurant in 1916, as did Burdine's in Miami; its Tea Roof was covered with a canopy.[36] At the Bon Marché of Brussels, that city's largest department store in 1930, a spacious roof restaurant afforded a fine view of the city.[37]

Department stores put their roofs to many other uses besides dining facilities, including children's play areas, skyline viewing, and employee solariums and gymnasiums. In 1907 Mitsukoshi opened a "Sky Garden" that featured a pond, fountain, plants, shrubs, and bonsais. As stores rebuilt after Japan's 1923 earthquake, many exploited their roofs for a wide variety of attractions, such as shrines, tea ceremony huts, children's playgrounds, and skating rinks.[38] Matsuzakaya installed a zoo with a lion and tiger in the 1920s. Filene's in Boston did the same in 1954, only to see it demolished in a hurricane that same year.[39] Shirokiya also had a rooftop zoo in the 1950s, as well as a monorail train, an ice cream stand, swings, and other playground equipment.[40] In the 1950s and 1960s American stores in warmer climates, such as Burdine's in Miami and Rich's in Atlanta, set up children's rides on their roofs during the Christmas season.

Most stores, however, located their children's play areas on upper floors inside the store. Like so many other services, playrooms and nurseries did not proliferate until the 1920s, although

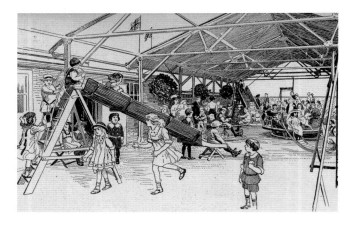

LEFT Roof terrace at Brussels' Bon Marché store, ca. 1930.

BELOW LEFT Families stroll through the garden atop the Mitsukoshi department store in Tokyo, ca. 1930.

BELOW RIGHT Band concert on the roof at Nordiska Kompaniet, Stockholm, 1950.

ABOVE Playground on the roof of T. Eaton, Toronto, as depicted in a store brochure early in the 20th century.

RIGHT Rooftop of the Emporium in San Francisco, featuring rides for children, 1947.

OPPOSITE A hydrogen balloon 48 feet (14.6 meters) in diameter was launched from the roof of Wanamaker's in New York in 1911.

Wanamaker's arranged a playroom "in charge of matrons" as early as 1889.[41] Shirokiya in Tokyo and Simpson's in Toronto had playrooms before 1910, and Marshall Field's exceptionally large facilities could care for three hundred to four hundred children.[42] Unfortunately, mothers often abused child-care services, leaving the store after depositing their child in the care of a nurse and sometimes failing to return by closing hours.[43] By the 1960s children's rooms were a rarity in department stores.[44]

Roof gardens, playgrounds, and restaurants all served to cultivate good will among shoppers and keep them from leaving the store prematurely, but they were seldom money-makers. Many other department-store services and amenities were more closely tied to commerce, either because they were fee based or because they directly facilitated sales. Such services included foreign-language interpreters (Paris stores of the early twentieth century even provided Esperanto speakers), mail order, package delivery, alteration and repair, and the like.[45]

Mail order and delivery were important aspects of the department-store industry, particularly in parts of the world where the population was spread thinly over a wide territory. The early success of Eaton's in Toronto was attributed to its catalog business, which was established in 1884, and Wanamaker's had what was described as a "mammoth" mail-order business in 1889.[46] Among the big stores of Paris, mail-order sales accounted for 30–40 percent of total volume in the 1880s and 1890s. Georges d'Avenel, an early analyst of the French stores, reported that in the early 1890s the Grands Magasins du Louvre and the Bon Marché each received an average of 4,000 orders by mail a day.[47] In 1894 the Bon Marché mailed out 1.5 million catalogs, 260,000 of which were sent outside the country.[48] By 1904 Eaton's was producing 1.3 million catalogs a year, while Harrods and Mitsukoshi were about to launch 24-hour-a-day telephone ordering services.[49] Eaton's mailed out about 11 million catalogs a year in the 1950s and continued its mail-order service until the 1970s.[50] Customers living in far-flung places around the world, as well as outside commuting distance to large cities in the early twentieth century were highly dependent upon mail order. It was said that every Canadian home contained a catalog from Simpson's, Eaton's, or some large department store in the United States and that many a young couple in British Columbia or Nova Scotia furnished their entire house this way.[51] The Galeries Lafayette sustained summer vacationers enjoying the sea air at Trouville by making special deliveries there. G. Fox would do the same several decades later for its Connecticut customers vacationing on the shore.[52] After moving to Yalta, Anton Chekhov relied so heavily on Moscow's Muir & Mirrielees that he named his puppies after the store.[53] Evidently British customers of Harrods became spoiled by how easy the store made it

to order things and have them delivered immediately. Harrods' director, Sir Richard Burbidge, acknowledged that wartime had a beneficial effect on the undisciplined shopping habits of some London women by forcing them to consolidate three separate food orders a day—for lunch, tea, and dinner—into one.[54]

Mail and telephone orders required large, highly organized delivery departments. By 1874 the Bon Marché employed one hundred people just to handle the 200,000 parcels it sent to the provinces and foreign countries.[55] Even shoppers who made their purchases in the store expected them to be delivered, a service that was free in most stores until the Depression. Mitsukoshi delivered packages to customers in Tokyo by bicycle messenger, but in 1903 acquired a French-made delivery van with the store's name on the side, a popular form of advertising for department stores.[56] By World War I the store offered free delivery to Tokyo's suburbs and as far as Yokohama, 18 miles (29 kilometers) away.[57] Until World War I Harrods made seven deliveries a day to London addresses and would deliver any purchase costing more than 61 cents for free.[58] A 1929 survey revealed that 90 percent of American stores offered free delivery.[59] Even when many stores eliminated free delivery during the Depression, others such as Marshall Field and Connecticut's G. Fox still maintained large delivery departments. Suburbanization and car travel eliminated the demand for delivery in most American stores, but in Japan, where many customers arrive by public transportation, delivery has continued to be an important service.[60]

Department stores often acted as brokers, agents, and contractors for a variety of goods and services that were somewhat outside the scope of their customary concerns. This included supplying armies with military goods. A. T. Stewart made a tidy profit by supplying the Union Army with underwear and uniforms during the Civil War.[61] They could furnish almost anything needed for a special event. Whiteleys in London was a pioneer in providing party requisites, including catered meals, tents, and prefab ballrooms complete with tables, chairs, china and linens, and Chinese lanterns. The store was known to have catered a dinner for 14,000 people on one occasion in the 1870s. It could also provide entertainment, ranging from ventriloquists, marionettes, and acrobats to performing dogs and birds. The forty-page for-hire section of the Whiteleys catalog included items such as portable rock gardens and grottoes.[62]

Whiteleys was also among the department stores that entered the real estate business. It would build and furnish a house to order, or completely furnish a rental flat for anyone wanting a temporary residence in London, taking back everything afterward.[63] Macy's put a prefab summer house on sale in the 1960s, completely furnished right down to toothbrushes.[64] Harrods, as well

ABOVE Catalog from Alle Città d'Italia, the Milan store owned by the Bocconi brothers that became La Rinascente in 1917.

RIGHT AND FAR RIGHT Eaton's "sea to sea" catalog, 1904, showing mechanical toys (right) and the cover (far right).

OPPOSITE Variously dated catalogs from Milan's Alle Città d'Italia, Berlin's N. Israel, Chicago's Mandel Brothers and Siegel-Cooper, and Paris's Grands Magasins du Louvre, plus a bill from Boston's R. H. White.

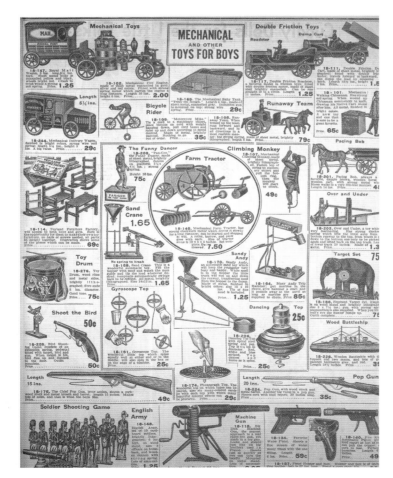

OPPOSITE, TOP
It took a while for urban department stores to adapt to rapid expansion in size and service, as demonstrated in this photograph of Woodward & Lothrop's use of the city sidewalks for sorting deliveries in 1924.

OPPOSITE, BOTTOM
The order department in the Bon Marché's Paris store.

OPPOSITE, INSET
Delivery tag used by Anthony Hordern, Sydney's "universal provider" store.

TOP Workers pull packages off of a chute in the delivery department at Marshall Field's.

ABOVE World War I–era motorbike-driven delivery vans at Harrods.

as a few U.S. stores, ran an Estate Office that sold properties.[65] In 1906, for instance, they offered a 9-acre estate in Upper Norwood, complete with fruit orchards, tennis lawns, and stables, and a house with 9 bedrooms and "3 good reception rooms."[66]

Most major stores offered decorating services, not only for residential customers but also for movie theaters, hotels, and other institutions, and B. Altman even decorated the Truman White House.[67] Other unusual services included large-scale outfitting. Some stores, such as Marshall Field's and Harrods, offered to outfit expeditions, hunting trips, and safaris.[68] In a 1906 advertisement Harrods declared that it had experts who could supply camp equipment, arms and ammunition, scientific instruments, mining tools, and a host of other items, and pack them for "Native Transport, Mule or Camel Loads." It had outfitted relief ships going to Argentina and the Antarctic as well as "Various Exploring, Mining, and Sporting Expeditions to Abyssinia, East and West Africa, Egypt, Sudan, Etc. Etc."[69]

Compared to outfitting expeditions, more conventional services offered by the big stores may seem tame, but they were appreciated by shoppers nonetheless. People flocked to the Grands Magasins du Louvre in the 1880s to be weighed on the store's scales by an "obligating official with a steel chain round his neck," who presented each person with a certificate of weight.[70] In the United States, mezzanine floors held bureaus such as travel agencies, post offices, ticket windows, telegraph offices, stock brokerages, watch repair desks, and pharmacies. Elsewhere in the store there were photo studios, teen clubs, bridal secretaries, custom dress salons, and beauty and barber shops. In the early twentieth century many department stores had lending libraries, such as the Wertheim store in Berlin, where George Grosz borrowed books when he first arrived in the city.[71] Always striving to outdo one another, some stores came up with unusual ideas such as a perfume fountain in which shoppers dipped their handkerchiefs at Mitsukoshi or a free wart-removal service at Selfridges.[72] Other novel services reflected exigencies of the times. The Depression inspired Selfridges to offer free cricket bat oiling, and the Anthony Hordern store in Sydney set up a free veterinary clinic.[73] With the threat of air raids looming as World War II approached, Harrods advertised it would gas-proof homes for $62 a room.[74]

Every Day a Circus

Fred Lazarus, founder of Federated Department Stores, felt that crowded aisles and hubbub were essential to convince customers that a department store was thriving. Silence and emptiness were fatal. "It's got to look busy, feel busy, be busy," he remarked in 1954, a time when U.S. department stores needed a boost.[75] He recommended hosting events such as international fairs with bagpipers and costumed folk dancers. This was not a new idea. As far back as the 1870s, clerks at the Bon Marché rolled counters aside to make room for evening lectures and concerts.[76] John Wanamaker, observing the crowds streaming to the Centennial Exposition of 1876 in Philadelphia, realized that there was a large and enthusiastic audience for patriotic and scientific programs. Among many other presentations, his store would host exhibits on the signing of the Constitution, the French Revolution, and colonial shoemaking.[77] Only in Germany, where there were campaigns against large-scale modern retailing, was a damper put on such promotional activities.[78]

Many department stores set aside space for auditoriums and galleries in which lectures, concerts, exhibits, and demonstrations were held. These events ranged from fashion shows to ikebana lessons to talks on child psychology or modern furniture design. Usually located on upper floors, large halls could comfortably hold hundreds. In 1908, before it was really much of a department store, Mitsukoshi boasted a performance stage and an art gallery. In its new store in the 1920s it installed a hall with a large stage for musicians and dancers and more than 600 seats.[79] In 1920 the Vandervoort store in St. Louis built a music hall for recitals, lectures, and Shakespearean performances.[80] The halls of G. Fox in Hartford, Connecticut, and Hudson's in Detroit could hold at least 800, while Wanamaker's Egyptian Room in Philadelphia seated 1,400.[81] Public entertainment venues inside stores, including movie theaters and sports facilities, proliferated in Japanese department stores such as Seibu, Matsuzakaya, Mitsukoshi, and Takashimaya, which became favored destinations for Sunday family outings.[82]

Presenting choral and symphonic concerts in department stores became quite popular in the nineteenth century. The Bon Marché sponsored two musical performances a year, beginning in 1873 and continuing for decades. Featuring singers from the Paris Opéra or employee choruses, they were held in the evening and open only to invited guests, becoming "something of a society event."[83] Sometimes concerts were intended simply to build good will and promote the store's reputation, but Wanamaker, one of the largest piano dealers in the entire country at the turn of the twentieth century, also used them as "the backdrop for one of the largest musical retailing enterprises in the United States."[84] A concert conducted by Richard Strauss in 1904 became part of the store's lore.[85]

BELOW Theater in the Crespin & Dufayel department store, Paris, ca. 1910.

BOTTOM When not in use for concerts, Wanamaker's Egyptian Room functioned as a piano showroom.

ABOVE The Bon Marché's clerks would spend hours removing all the merchandise and display cases from the selling floors to ready them for concerts, 1887.

OPPOSITE
Artist's conception of a gala event celebrating the 1924 reopening of Printemps, after the catastrophic fire of 1921. The men and women guests are dressed in formal wear.

The daily organ concerts given at Wanamaker's throughout the twentieth century may have been unique in the annals of department-store history, but many stores hired orchestras to play for special events such as Spring and Fall fashion shows or anniversary celebrations. Ehrich Brothers in New York City, believed to be the first U.S. store to hold a fashion show, hired a band to accompany the event in 1903.[86] Many stores formed choral groups, partly to entertain shoppers in the store on holidays but also to improve workers' morale. Mitsukoshi organized boy employees into a band that often gave free concerts, playing both Japanese music and that of other nations. Spectators in 1918 were delighted to see the boys playing bagpipes dressed in kilts.[87]

Department stores hosted so many elaborate exhibits that they were often compared favorably to public museums, which sought to follow their model of display techniques and public accessibility.[88] Marshall Field was called "Chicago's Third Museum."[89] Mitsukoshi considered its stores "cultural media through which it aspires to promote international cultural exchanges."[90] Its exhibits have covered everything from historic artifacts to natural wonders and scientific discoveries. Moscow's universal provider in Soviet times, the state-run GUM, presented shoppers with an exhibit of birds and dogs in 1925 that it proclaimed was "something never seen prior to the revolution."[91]

Airplanes were a huge attraction in department stores in the first several decades of the twentieth century. Selfridges displayed the plane that Louis Blériot flew across the English Channel in 1909, attracting 150,000 spectators in the first few days of the exhibit.[92] The store also displayed Amy Johnson's Gipsy Moth airplane, Alan Cobham's seaplane, which had landed on the Thames in 1926, and the plane flown by Lord Clydesdale in the first flight over Mount Everest, which took place in 1933.[93] The Galeries Lafayette created a sensation in 1919 by having Jules Vedrines perform a pancake landing on the store's roof, a stunt that was somewhat deflated when the police forbade the pilot to fly the airplane off the roof. Vedrines had to disassemble the plane and lower it by elevator.[94] A week-long airplane exhibit at Kaufmann's in Pittsburgh in 1928 presented planes, aircraft gear, demonstrations that simulated the feeling of flight, and lectures by famous aviators.[95]

Art exhibitions not only generated crowds but also enhanced stores' prestige as cultural centers. Although some of the art may not have lived up to its billing, at times the shows were quite impressive. In many cases the paintings and sculptures on display in a store's art gallery were for sale, even as they added cachet to the store. About 1874 the Bon Marché opened a picture gallery in a room with magnificent frescoes and works of sculpture; artists were invited to exhibit their paintings for up to six weeks.[96] A gallery that opened with much fanfare at the Jordan Marsh store in Boston in 1894 was likewise filled with works intended for sale.[97]

LEFT Lord & Taylor offered a special sale of jewelry and small art objects acquired from the Soviet government in 1933.

OPPOSITE, TOP Even before it grew into a full-fledged department store, the Mitsukoshi dry goods store held art exhibitions such as this one, ca. 1910.

OPPOSITE, BOTTOM In 1933 Nordiska Kompaniet presented an exhibit detailing the way of life of the indigenous reindeer-herding Sami people of northern Sweden.

In the twentieth century department stores ventured into modern art. The Leonhard Tietz store in Düsseldorf sold works by Max Liebermann and Wilhelm Trübner in 1909.[98] Other stores gave contemporary artists a place to show their work when museums, many of which still had not embraced the new trends in art, rejected them. Selfridge presented a *salon des refusés* of works rejected by the Royal Academy shortly after his store opened in London,[99] and a similar exhibit was mounted by the Rothschild store on Chicago's State Street in 1921.[100] Gimbels toured an exhibition of works by contemporary artists, including Fernand Léger, Albert Gleizes, Jean Metzinger, Pierre Dumont, and Jacques Villon in 1913, and in 1918 Carson Pirie Scott exhibited Robert Henri, George Bellows, William Glackens, and John Sloan.[101]

As many department-store founders and executives were themselves major art collectors, they often took the opportunity to display their own collections in the stores. John Wanamaker exhibited pieces from his private collection, which included works by Constable, Titian, Turner, and many other well-known artists.[102] Morton D. May, president and chief executive officer of the May Department Stores, displayed over 1,200 pieces from his collection of ancient Greek and Roman art at Hecht's in Washington, D.C., one of the May Company stores, in 1965. Featuring gold jewelry, weapons, bronzes, and marble sculptures, the exhibition ran concurrently with an import fair and no doubt enhanced it.[103] Similar motives must have prompted the Düsseldorf Kaufhof store's collaboration with a local art gallery to sell works by artists such as Victor Vasarely instead of the calendar-style framed pictures that it usually sold in the 1960s.[104]

ABOVE Visitors crowd around to view replicas of swords of state on exhibit at Eaton's in Toronto in 1937.

In Japanese stores art exhibits have been so extensive and frequent that the stores have truly achieved museum status. In the 1910s the Mitsukoshi store was known for exhibits of exquisite kimonos, lacquerware, and porcelain.[105] But it wasn't until after World War II that most stores became serious about showing art. In the 1950s a visitor might have had half a dozen exhibits to choose from in a single store, ranging from Noh masks by a famed sculptor to contemporary pottery to eighteenth-century woodcuts.[106] A 1961 story in the *New York Times* commented, "It was a poor department store that does not have at least one exhibition going every day."[107] Attempting to win a reputation as a patron of the arts, Seibu co-sponsored significant art exhibits in the 1960s and 1970s, attracting hundreds of thousands of viewers. A Gauguin exhibit at the Ikebukuro store in 1969 brought in 400,000 spectators, as did a Millet show the following year, and Renoir drew 550,000 in 1971.[108]

Japan might be thought of as the last florescence of a strong department-store culture. Yet if Japanese department stores are regarded as "vertical shopping malls," then it would appear that

Art Exhibition held in the Mitsukoshi Store, Tokyo. 三越美術工藝品展覽會陳列場

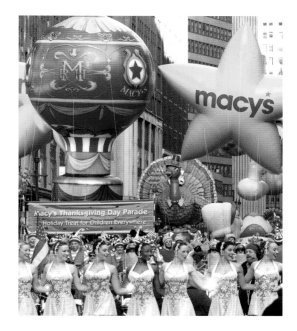

shopping malls are another sign of the vitality of the circuslike traditions of classic downtown department stores. Their atriums, food courts, kiosk-filled concourses, and seasonal events give continuity to the notion of shopping as entertainment.

Of all the hoopla and circuslike events initiated by department stores, none has become more cherished by the public than the holiday parade. It has thrived particularly in North America. Who can say for sure when the idea first struck a department store to have Santa Claus arrive at the store with the utmost spectacle? There may have been a few parades in the 1890s, but it was in the early twentieth century that they became major events on the big stores' calendars. Eaton's held its first Santa parade in Toronto in 1905, and by mid-century it had become one of the largest, if not the largest.[109] Holiday parades sponsored by department stores flourished in the 1920s, not only at Christmas but also at Easter and sometimes Halloween. Gimbels in Philadelphia began its Christmas parade in 1920, and it probably rivaled Eaton's. By the mid-1920s Eaton's parade had spread to Montreal, and department stores in most major U.S. cities hosted their own versions, including Macy's in New York City, Hudson's in Detroit, Bamberger's in Newark, and Nugent's in St. Louis. Usually held on Thanksgiving Day, they typically ended at the store, where the king of the elves mounted a throne atop the front marquee and invited the crowd to the unveiling of the Christmas windows and the official opening of Toyland.[110] (The fact that customers could not actually visit Toyland until the following day was an everlasting source of dismay to retailers.) In 1924, the first year of Macy's parade, puppeteer and illustrator Tony Sarg created a marionette show, Fairy Frolics of Wondertown, for the store's windows.[111]

The first Macy's Thanksgiving Day parade attracted only about 10,000 spectators and was dwarfed by Eaton's and Gimbels' events in Philadelphia. In 1928, when Sarg's helium-filled balloons first appeared, Macy's crowd had increased ten-fold, but it wasn't until after World War II that Macy's, though still in competition with Eaton's and Hudson's, would move toward becoming a parade for all Americans, stimulated by the film *Miracle on 34th Street*, which contained scenes from the 1946 parade. Nationwide TV coverage in the 1950s also spread the fame of Macy's parade. While many stores gave up their parades in the 1960s, 1970s, and 1980s, Macy's persisted and cemented its status as a national institution. Since 2001 it has drawn about three million live spectators annually, with many more millions watching on TV.

ABOVE The workshop in which Macy's floats are created, 1980.

LEFT Harrods' bagpipers parade in front of the store, ca. 1995.

Postscript

In 1932 economist Paul Nystrom observed that department stores had become cornerstones of modern civilization.[1] Like newspapers, electricity, bustling urban centers, and public transportation, they were so much a product of the industrial era that it's hard to avoid the question, Are they anachronisms today? Given the number of stores that closed in the latter part of the last century, particularly in downtown centers of American cities, it would seem that the big stores with their solid architecture and soaring halls are a thing of the past, having lived on well beyond their life expectancy.

Many of the stores mentioned in this book have merged with others, while some are gone for good, such as Wanamaker's, the Samaritaine, and the Takashimaya store in New York City. And yet...throughout their long history department stores have demonstrated an amazing ability to reinvent themselves. They moved branches into malls, and when malls began to lag, due in part to consumers' wish to save time, they created efficient Internet shopping services. Over time many stores have cut back on the number of departments. The emphasis on household goods, once central to the merchandise base of most stores, has been minimized, whereas ready-to-wear clothing and accessories—always primary in French stores—have assumed much greater importance. Some stores are now considering bringing back toy departments. Some are offering more special events or taking on a local character that reflects their geographical milieu. Others, such as the Bon Marché, have decided to go after the luxury market. Even during the recent recession department stores around the world showed a determination to survive.

The future is difficult—and somewhat foolish—to predict. Clearly, it can still be said that department stores demonstrate that shopping is much more than the mere acquisition of goods. They are more than warehouses filled with goods; they are also gathering places and multi-use cultural spaces that create a sense of place. Should they disappear, it is difficult to imagine what could take their place in modern culture.

Notes

WONDERS OF THE WORLD

1 Mary Very, "Au Bon Marché," *The Independent*, 29 July 1875, 6.
2 "Marshall Field & Co.," *Fortune*, October 1936, 79.
3 William Lancaster, *The Department Store: A Social History* (London, New York: Leicester University Press, 1995), 201.
4 "Marshall Field, the Store," *Fortune*, December 1945, 146.
5 George H. Johnston, "Departed Glory of the Ginza," *The Melbourne Argus*, 8 September 1945, 7.
6 Michael S. Smith, "Putting France in the Chandlerian Framework," *The Business History Review*, 71(1), Spring 1998, 52.
7 Herbert Adams Gibbons, *John Wanamaker*, vol. 2 (New York: Harper & Bros., 1926), 189.
8 Charles Dickens, Jr., "The Universal Provider," *All the Year Round*, 481, 16 February 1878, 85.
9 Sam Jameson, "Tokyo Store Takes Care of Customers, Even After Death," *Los Angeles Times*, 10 March 1977, B14.
10 John J. Daly, "The Department Store: Can the Book Trade Compete with It?" *The Publishers' Weekly*, 1355, 15 January 1898, 60.
11 Louis Parnes, *Planning Stores That Pay* (New York: F. W. Dodge Corporation, 1948), 71.
12 Louise Young, "Marketing the Modern Department Stores, Consumer Culture, and the New Middle Class in Interwar Japan," *International Labor and Working-Class History*, 55, Spring 1999, 66.
13 Theo Child, "The Women's Paradise," *Lippincott's Magazine*, November 1884, 515.

A WORLD OF DEPARTMENT STORES

1 Young, 1999, 61.
2 Paul O. Grokë, "How Japanese Department Stores Are Meeting the Challenge of a Rapidly Changing Environment," *Journal of Retailing*, 48(3), Fall 1972, 79.
3 Paul Greenlagh, *Ephemeral Vistas: The Expositions Universelles, Great Exhibitions and World's Fairs*, 1851–1939 (Manchester, U.K.: Manchester University Press, 1988), 15.
4 John William Ferry, *A History of the Department Store* (New York: Macmillan, 1960), 260, 205.
5 Michael Barry Miller, *The Bon Marché: Bourgeois Culture and the Department Store, 1869–1920* (Princeton, NJ: Princeton University Press, 1981), 45.
6 Joseph Siry, *Carson Pirie Scott: Louis Sullivan and the Chicago Department Store* (Chicago: University of Chicago Press, 1988), 41.
7 Joseph Siry, "Louis Sullivan's Building for John D. Van Allen and Son," *Journal of the Society of Architectural Historians*, 49(1), 1990, 81.
8 "A New Enterprise. The Des Moines Department Store," *The Midwestern*, 1(2), October 1906, 67.
9 "Joined to Fight the Big Stores," *Chicago Daily Times*, 18 February 1897, 7.
10 Alexandre Weill, *Les Grands magasins de Paris et les moyens de les combattre*, 3rd ed. (Paris: Paul Sévin, 1891), 12.
11 Joel A. Tarr, "The Chicago Anti-Department Store Crusade of 1897," *Journal of the Illinois State Historical Society*, 64(2), 1971; Helmut Frei, *Tempel der Kauflust: Eine Geschichte der Warenhauskultur* (Leipzig: Edition Leipzig, 1997), 13, 156–58; Joy L. Santink, *Timothy Eaton and the Rise of His Department Store* (Toronto: University of Toronto Press, 1990), 181.
12 Katherine G. Busbey, *Home Life in America* (New York: The Macmillan Company, 1910), 163–64.
13 Leon Harris, *Merchant Princes: An Intimate History of Jewish Families Who Built Great Department Stores* (New York: Kodansha International, 1994), 128.
14 Paul Dehn, *Die Grossbazare und Massenzweiggeschäfte* (Berlin: Trowitzsch, 1899), 66. Author's translation.
15 Simone Ladwig-Winters, "The Attack on Berlin Department Stores after 1933," in *Probing the Depths of German Antisemitism*, ed. David Bankier (New York: Berghahn Books, 2000); Thomas R. H. Havens, *Architecture of Affluence: The Tsutsumi Family and the Seibu-Saison Enterprise in Twentieth-Century Japan* (Cambridge, MA: Harvard University Press, 1994), 61.
16 Werner Sombart, *Der Moderne Kapitalismus* (Leipzig: Verlag Von Duncker & Humblot, 1902), 397.
17 Hrant Pasdermadjian, *The Department Store, Its Origins, Evolution and Economics* (London: Newman Books, 1954), 3–4; Helen Rich Norton, *A Textbook on Retail Selling* (Boston, New York: Ginn & Company 1919), 9–10.
18 Miller, 1981, 26–30.
19 Philip G. Nord, *Paris Shopkeepers and the Politics of Resentment* (Princeton, NJ: Princeton University Press, 1986), 63.
20 Julius Hirsch, "Department Stores Abroad," *The Living Age*, September 1928, 57.
21 "French Department Stores' Expanding," *Wall Street Journal*, 20 December 1928, 4.
22 Paul Nystrom, *The Economics of Retailing* (New York: The Ronald Press, 1919), 249.
23 Harry E. Resseguie, "Alexander Turney Stewart and the Development of the Department Store, 1823–1876," *The Business History Review*, 39(3), Autumn 1965, 301.
24 Ralph M. Hower, *History of Macy's of New York 1858–1919* (Cambridge, MA: Harvard University Press 1943), 144.
25 Paul H. Nystrom, *The Economics of Retailing*, 3rd ed. (New York: The Ronald Press, 1932), 141.
26 Nystrom, 1919, 248.
27 "Modern Department Store Does Tremendous Business," *Wall Street Journal*, 28 November 1921, 1; Sombart, 1902, 397–98.
28 Robert Hendrickson, *The Grand Emporiums: The Illustrated History of America's Great Department Stores* (New York: Stein and Day, 1979), 58.
29 Nystrom, 1919, 249; Talcott Williams, "The Great Department Store; Men, Mechanism, Methods; Managers and Management of the Modern Store," *The Booklover's Magazine*, I(V), May 1903, 453.
30 "Modern Department Stores Does a Tremendous Business," 1921, 1.
31 Pasdermadjian, 1954, 36-37.
32 Rudolf Lenz, *Karstadt: Ein deutscher Warenhauskonzern, 1920-1950* (Stuttgart: Deutsche Verlags-Anstalt, 1995), 46.
33 Christine Frederick, *Selling Mrs. Consumer* (New York: The Business Bourse, 1929), 311–12.
34 Leonard Sloane, "In Philadelphia, Nearly Everyone Can Find Strawbridge & Clothier," *New York Times*, 18 December 1965, 39; Leonard Sloane, "On State Street, It's Still Marshall Field," *New York Times*, 21 December 1965, 55.
35 Lancaster, 1995, 24.
36 Ferry, 1960, 191.
37 Pasdermadjian, 1954, 6-7; Lancaster, 1995, 69-70.
38 Julia Hood and B. S. Yamey, "The Middle-Class Co-Operative Retailing Societies in London, 1864-1900," *Oxford Economic Papers* (New Series), 9(3), October 1957, 309.
39 Tim Coles, "Department Stores as Retail Innovations in Germany: A Historical-Geographical Perspective on the Period 1870 to 1914," in *Cathedrals of Consumption: The European Department Store, 1850-1939*, ed. Geoffrey Crossick and Serge Jaumain (Aldershot, U.K.: Ashgate, 1999), 73.
40 Hood and Yamey, 1957, 318, fn. 1.
41 Pasdermadjian, 1954, 7, 47–48.
42 Ferry, 1960, 191.
43 Sombart, 1902, 397–98.
44 Lancaster, 1995, 80; personal communication, Sebastian Wormell, Harrods' archivist, May 11, 2010.
45 Georg Tietz, *Hermann Tietz: Geschichte einer Familie und ihrer Warenhäuser* (Stuttgart: Deutsche Verlags-Anstalt, 1965), 53–54.
46 Lenz, 1995, 51.
47 Coles, 1999, 73.
48 Paul Göhre, *Das Warenhaus* (Frankfurt am Main: Literarische Anstalt/Rütten & Loening, 1907), 89–90; Siegfried Gerlach, *Das Warenhaus in Deutschland. Seine Entwicklung bis zum ersten Weltkrieg in historisch-geographischer Sicht* (Stuttgart: Franz Steiner Verlag, 1988), 62.
49 Coles, 1999, 85.
50 Irene Guenther, *Nazi Chic? Fashioning Women in the Third Reich* (Oxford: Berg Publishers, 2004), 163.
51 "Salman Schocken Is Dead at 81," *New York Times*, 8 August 1959, 17; Anthony David, *The Patron: A Life of Salman Schocken 1877–1959* (New York: Metropolitan Books/Henry Holt, 2003), 209.
52 Hirsch, 1928, 57.
53 Janet Ward Lungstrum, "The Display Window: Designs and Desires of Weimar Consumerism," *New German Critique*, 76, Winter 1999, 136; Frei, 1997, 124.
54 Lenz, 1995, 176–79, 204, 329–30.
55 Giichi Fukami, "Japanese Department Stores," *The Journal of Marketing*, 18(1), July 1953, 41.
56 Donica Belisle, "Negotiating Paternalism. Women and Canada's Largest Department Stores, 1890–1960," *Journal of Women's History*, 19(1), Spring 2007, 60–61.
57 Dale Miller and Bill Merrilees, "Fashion and Commerce: A Historical Perspective on Australian Fashion Retailing 1880–1920," *International Journal of Retail and Distribution*, 32(8/9), 2004, 397, 394; Hordern's advertisement, *The Sydney Morning Herald*, 18 September 1887.
58 Ferry, 1960, 335–39.
59 Lancaster, 1995, 299.
60 Marshall L. Goldman, "Retailing in the Soviet Union," *The Journal of Marketing*, 24(4), April 1960, 13–14.
61 Frei, 1997, 134–35.
62 Pasdermadjian, 1954, 66.
63 Frei, 1997, 16–17.
64 Giancarlo Rivazzi, 'Retailing in a Developing Economy—Italy," *Journal of Retailing*, Spring 1967, 39–40.
65 Frei, 1997, 20–21.
66 "Stewart, and the Dry Goods Trade of New York," *The Continental Monthly*, II(V), November 1862, 531.
67 Reginald Pound, *Selfridge: A Biography* (London: Heinemann, 1960), 122.
68 "Paris Mourns Mme. Cognacq, Friend of Poor," *New York Times*, 31 January 1926, X16.
69 Junius Henri Browne, *The Great Metropolis* (Hartford, CT: American Publishing Company, 1869), 293.
70 Havens, 1994, 64.
71 Carpenter, 1909, 3; Pierre N. Beringer, "The House of Mitsui," *Overland Monthly*, LV(1), January 1910, 90–93.
72 Robert Proctor, "Constructing the Retail Monument: The Parisian Department Store and Its Property, 1855–1914," *Urban History*, 33(3), 2006, 399.
73 Tietz, 1965, 139.
74 Browne, 1869, 289.
75 *The Scotch-Irish in America* (Nashville and Dallas: The Scotch-Irish Society of America, 1900), 217.
76 "Marshall Field," *Chicago Daily Times*, 17 January 1906, 8.
77 "Stewart, Alexander Turney," in *The National Cyclopedia of American Biography*, vol. 7 (New York: James T. White & Company, 1897), 352.
78 Tietz, 1965, 73.
79 "Salman Schocken Is Dead at 81," 1959, 17.
80 "Paris Merchant Loses $3,000,000 in a Panic," *New York Times*, 1 August 1905, 2.
81 Karl Baedeker, *Paris and Its Environs* (Leipzig: Karl Baedeker Publisher, London: T. Fisher Unwin, and New York: Charles Scribner's Sons, 1913), 174.
82 Ferry, 1960, 336–37.
83 Harris, 1994, 125.
84 "Paris Mourns Mme. Cognacq, Friend of Poor," 1926, X16.
85 "Parisian Builds a New Town in France," *New York Times*, 2 August 1903, 17.
86 "Chauchard Funeral Jeered and Hissed," *New York Times*, 11 June 1909, 4.
87 "The Case of Henry Siegel," *New York Times*, 26 November 1914, 12; Charles William Smith, *International Commercial and Financial Gambling in 'Options and Futures'* (London: P. S. King and Son, 1906), 26.
88 "Shot Down by Alleged Son," *Boston Daily Globe*, 25 January 1907, 9.
89 "Stewart, Alexander Turney," 1897, 352.
90 "John Wanamaker," in *Illustrated Philadelphia*, 2nd ed. (New York: American Publishing and Engraving Co., 1889), 118.
91 "Paris Mourns Mme. Cognacq, Friend of Poor," 1926, X16.
92 Tom Mahoney and Rita Hession, *Public Relations for Retailers* (New York: The Macmillan Co.), 1949, 186.
93 Harris, 1994, 45.
94 Tietz, 1965, 65–66, 174–75.
95 Belisle, 2007, 61.
96 Frank G. Carpenter, "Shopping in Stocking Feet in Japan's Biggest Store," *Boston Daily Globe Sunday Magazine*, 24 January 1909, 3.
97 Harris, 1994, 53; "Paris Merchant Loses $3,000,000 in a Panic," 1905, 2.

THE ENDLESS SHOPPING SPREE

1 Resseguie, 1965, 303; Pasdermadjian, 1954, 4.
2 David Hamlin, "Romanticism, Spectacle, and a Critique of Wilhelmine Consumer Capitalism," *Central European History*, 38(2), 2005, 254.
3 Margaret J. M. Sweat, *Highways of Travel; or A Summer in Europe* (Boston: Walker, Wise and Company, 1859), 323.
4 Lancaster, 1995, 75.
5 Clemens Wischermann, "Placing Advertising in the Modern Cultural History of the City," in *Advertising and the European City: Historical Perspectives*, ed. Clemens Wischermann and Elliott Shore (Aldershot, England: Ashgate, 2000), 1.
6 Proctor, 2006, 395.
7 "Shopping in London," *Boston Daily Globe*, 11 July 1909, 24.
8 Frank G. Carpenter, "Best Managed City of Europe," *Boston Daily Globe*, 22 March 1903, 46.
9 Stanhope Sams, "Department Stores," in *Selling Wearing Apparel in Japan*, Dept. of Commerce Special Agents Series, No. 130 (Washington, D.C.: GPO, 1917), 40.
10 Marjorie L. Hilton, "Retailing the Revolution: The State Department Store (GUM) and Soviet Society in the 1920s," *Journal of Social History*, 37(4), 2004, 957.
11 Child, 1884, 517.
12 "America To-Day. Yankee Department Stores," *The Adelaide Advertiser*, 29 June 1905, 9.
13 "Paris. The Ruling Passion—Paris in the Dark," *New York Evangelist*, 29 September 1870, 2.
14 Busbey, 1910, 164.
15 "Paris Shops. The Great Dry Goods Emporiums of the French Capital," *San Francisco Bulletin*, 15 May 1882, 1.
16 Jennifer Dunning, "Browsing in Phantom Emporiums Along the Ladies Mile," *New York Times*, 5 November 1976, 64.
17 Russell Lewis, "Everything Under One Roof: World's Fairs and Department Stores in Paris and Chicago," *Chicago History*, 12(3), Fall 1983, 39; Erika Diana Rappaport, *Shopping for Pleasure: Women in the Making of London's West End* (Princeton, NJ; Princeton University Press, 2000), 143.
18 "Came to See the Sights," *New York Times*, 20 May 1900, 12.
19 Mary E. Parker Bouligny, *Bubbles and Ballast* (Baltimore: Kelly, Piet & Company, 1871), 87.
20 Child, 1884, 515.
21 Edmund Buckley, "Artistic Aspects of America's Greatest Store," *Fine Arts Journal*, April 1908, 196.
22 Parnes, 1948, 256.
23 "The Fall of the House of Stewart," *New York Times*, 28 August 1896, 4.
24 Twain, 1907, 204; Siry, 1988, 39.
25 Lucy H. Hooper, "Parisian Shops and Shopping," *Appleton's Journal*, 11 April 1874, 466.
26 "The Shops at Christmas Time," *Warehousemen and Drapers' Trade Journal*, 16 December 1874, 644.
27 Parnes, 1948, 166–67.
28 "Harrods Banks on Tradition," *Los Angeles Times*, 24 December 1981, A4.
29 Young, 1999, 59–60.
30 Havens, 1994, 65, 79.
31 "Opening of the Holiday Season; Review of the Leading Metropolitan Toy Departments," *Playthings*, 6(11), November 1908, 52.
32 *I.C.S. Reference Library: Advertisement Display, Mediums, Retail Management, Department-Store Management* (Scranton, PA: International Textbook Company, 1909), 39; "What Does It Cost to Keep a Customer?" *New York Times Sunday Magazine*, 31 March 1912, 13.
33 Alfred Fantil [Fantl], "Experiences of a Buyer," *American Magazine*, vol. 95, April 1923, 220.
34 William Leach, *Land of Desire: Merchants, Power, and the Rise of a New American Culture* (New York: Vintage Books, 1993), 337.
35 "Round the Shops. Varied Gifts for Christmas. Attractions for Children," *The Times*, 8 December 1932, 8.
36 Lloyd Wendt and Herman Kogan, *Give the Lady What She Wants!: The Story of Marshall Field & Company* (Chicago: Rand McNally Co., 1952), 336–37.
37 Miller, 1981, 71.
38 Betty Blythe, "An Intimate Feminine View," *The Indianapolis Star*, 10 January 1913, 10.
39 Tietz, 1965, 68–69.
40 Child, 1884, 518–19; John Henry Hepp, *The Middle-Class City: Transforming Space and Time in Philadelphia, 1876–1927* (Philadelphia: University of Pennsylvania Press, 2003), 84–85.
41 Child, 1884, 519.
42 Kenneth Collins, *Retail Selling and the New Order* (New York: Greenberg, 1934), 87.
43 Stanley Marcus, *Minding the Store* (Boston: Little, Brown & Co., 1974), 210.
44 Joseph H. Appel, *The Business Biography of John Wanamaker* (New York: AMS Press, 1970, reprint of 1930 ed.), 101.
45 Dehn, 1899, 9–18.
46 Annie Marion MacLean, "Two Weeks in Department Stores," *American Journal of Sociology*, 4(6), May 1899, 725.
47 William Nelson Taft, *Department-Store Advertising* (Scranton, PA: International Textbook Co., 1929), 24.
48 Ibid.
49 Leach, 1993, 23.
50 Robert R. Henry, "The Carriage Trade Myth," *Journal of Retailing*, 38(3), Fall 1962.
51 "Department Stores," *Current Literature*, XXII(6), December 1897, 485.
52 Frei, 1997, 153–54; Robert Proctor, "Selling Art Nouveau in the Capital: The Nancy School in Paris," *Art on the Line*, 1(3), 2007, 2.
53 Pasdermadjian, 1954, 3–5; Norton, 1919, 9–10.
54 Lancaster, 1995, 21.
55 "Preparations for the New Year," *Warehousemen and Drapers' Trade Journal*, 3 January 1874, 4.

56 "Vidi's Note Book. No. II. Miscellaneous Goods," *Warehousemen and Drapers' Trade Journal*, 23 May 1874, 326.

57 Forrest Crissey, *Since Forty Years Ago* (Chicago: The Fair, 1915), unnumbered pages.

58 Dickens, 1878, 84.

59 "The Universal Provider," *Kansas City Star*, 12 August 1887, 2.

60 "Dry Goods and Fish," *Los Angeles Times*, 24 August 1897, 10.

61 Appel, 1970, 97.

62 "Marshall Field & Co.," in *Commercial and Architectural Chicago* (Chicago: G. W. Orear, Publisher, 1887), 203; Wendt and Kogan, 1952, 303.

63 Norman Patterson, "Evolution of a Departmental Store," *The Canadian Magazine*, XXVII(5), September 1906, 433.

64 Coles, 1999, 75.

65 William Leach, "Strategists of Display and the Production of Desire," in *Consuming Visions*, ed. Simon J. Bronner (New York: Norton, 1989), 117; Pound, 1960, 100.

66 Dehn, 1899, 81.

67 "So You're Going to Bloomingdale's!" *The New Yorker*, 8 December 1928, 23.

68 Ladwig-Winters, 2000, 253.

69 Jennifer Merin, "Stalking Trophies in World's Shops," *Los Angeles Times*, 6 March 1983, G22.

70 Alice Siegert, "A Food Paradise in the Shadow of the Berlin Wall," *Chicago Times*, 9 June 1980, E3.

71 Frei, 1997, 153; Gerlach, 1988, 59.

72 "The Department Store: Can the Book Trade Compete with It?" *The Publishers' Weekly*, 15 January 1898, 58, 60.

73 Dehn, 1899, 21.

74 Marc Henry, *Beyond the Rhine. Memories of Art and Life in Germany Before the War* (New York: Dodd Mead and Company, 1918), 145.

75 James B. Morrow, "Explains How Books Are Sold," *Boston Daily Globe Sunday Magazine*, 4 August 1912, 5.

76 David, 2003, 99.

77 Ferry, 1960, 221.

78 "Defense of Big Stores," *Chicago Daily Times*, 15 March 1897, 5.

79 Young, 1999, 59.

80 Santink, 1990, 68.

81 Martha Sonntag Bradley, *ZCMI, America's First Department Store* (Salt Lake City: Zion's Cooperative Mercantile Intitution, 1991), 44.

82 David, 2003, 171.

83 James M. Wood, *Halle's: Memoirs of a Family Department Store (1891–1982)* (Cleveland: Geranium Press, 1987), 80.

84 Filene's postcard, ca. 1906, author's collection; Dean Krimmel, "Merchant Princes and Their Palaces: The Emergence of Department Stores in Baltimore," in *Enterprising Emporiums: The Jewish Department Stores of Downtown Baltimore* (Baltimore: The Jewish Museum of Maryland, 2001), 28.

85 Cartoon by "Opper," *Puck*, 7 October 1896, 16.

86 "The Universal Provider," 1887, 2.

87 Leach, 1993, 23.

88 "Live Horses at Six and Seven-eighths Cents a Pound," *Printers' Ink*, 13 April 1922, 76.

89 Junnosuke Ofusa, "Weddings and Zoos in Tokyo Stores," *New York Times*, 24 January 1972, 42.

90 Child, 1884, 517.

91 Sarah Payson, *Fern Leaves from Fanny's Port-Folio*, 2nd ser. (Auburn and Buffalo, N.Y.: Miller, Orton & Mulligan, 1854), 340.

92 Edward Crapsey, "A Monument of Trade," *The Galaxy*, January 1870, 100.

93 Wendt and Kogan, 1952, 223.

94 Nystrom, 1919, 261.

95 Attributed to hotel operator Simeon Ford, speaking of the Waldorf-Astoria, cited in Lew Hahn, *Stores, Merchants and Customers* (New York: Fairchild Publications, 1952), 23.

96 Ladwig-Winters, 2000, 249.

97 *The History of Lord & Taylor* (New York: Lord & Taylor, 1926).

98 Mark Stevens, *"Like No Other Store in the World": The Inside Story of Bloomingdale's* (New York: Thomas Y. Crowell, 1979), 78.

99 Child, 1884, 519.

100 "Articles de Paris," *Harper's Bazaar*, 29 February 1868, 282.

101 E. F. H. M., "The Christmas Holidays in Paris," *Christian Union*, 20 December 1888, 720; Cecily Sidgwick, *Home Life in Germany* (New York: The Macmillan Co., 1908), 167.

102 Tobe, "Women's Apparel," in *Twenty-Five Years of Retailing*, 1911–1936, ed. John Hahn (New York: National Retail Dry Goods Association, 1936), 155.

103 Nancy J. Troy, *Modernism and the Decorative Arts in France; Art Nouveau to Le Corbusier* (New Haven: Yale University Press, 1991), 170, 177.

104 Proctor, 2007, 4–5.

105 Cilla Robach, "Design for Modern People," in *Utopia and Reality: Modernity in Sweden 1900–1960*, ed. Cecilia Widenheim (New Haven: Yale University Press, 2002), 200.

106 Child, 1884, 518–19; Robert C. Williams, *Russian Art and American Money* (Cambridge, MA: Harvard University Press, 1980).

107 Williams, 1980, 221.

108 Gimbels advertisement, *New York Times*, 2 February 1941, 48.

109 Geoffrey T. Hellman, "Onward & Upward with the Arts. Monastery for Sale," *The New Yorker*, 1 February 1941, 37.

110 Marcus, 1974, 177.

111 Brian Moeran, "The Birth of the Japanese Department Store," in *Asian Department Stores*, ed. Kerrie L. MacPherson (Honolulu: University of Hawaii Press, 1998), 154.

112 William Henry Beable, *Commercial Russia* (New York: The Macmillan Company, 1919), 161–62.

113 Alfred Fantl, "'Styling' the American Department Store with Foreign Merchandise," *Journal of Retailing*, 2(3), October 1926, 5.

114 C. R. Richards, *Art in Industry* (New York: The Macmillan Co., 1922), 2.

115 Eaton's advertisement, *The Lethbridge Herald*, 10 October 1944, back page.

116 "Studying Yankee Emporiums. Mr. Tietz of Germany Here to Learn About Our Big Department Stores," *New York Times*, 31 January 1907, 5.

117 Edwin N. Gunsaulus, "Department Stores at Singapore," in *Commerce Reports*, vol. 1, no. 62, 16 March 1917, 1006.

118 Mrs. Robert Noble, "A Tour Round the West-End Shops," *The Strand Magazine*, December 1908, 146.

119 George O'Brien, "Good Design Is Stressed by Italian Store Chain," *New York Times*, 10 February 1964, 30.

120 Milton Bracker, "Paris Store Has a Taste of America," *New York Times*, 16 March 1961, 41.

121 Debora Silverman, *Selling Culture* (New York: Pantheon Books, 1986), 27.

122 Philip J. Reilly, *Old Masters of Retailing* (New York: Fairchild Publications, Inc., 1966), 116.

123 Susan A. Goldenberg, "Americanizing Canadian Retailers," *New York Times*, 28 July 1985, F4.

BUILDING TO IMPRESS

1 Meredith L. Clausen, "The Department Store—Development of the Type," *Journal of Architectural Education*, 39(1) Autumn 1985, 20.

2 Proctor, 2006, 394–95.

3 David Cheney, "The Department Store as a Cultural Form," *Theory, Culture & Society*, 1(3), 1983, 25.

4 Bernard Marrey, *Les grands magasins des origines à 1939* (Paris: Librairies Picard, 1979), fig. 107, 112.

5 Proctor, 2006, 394.

6 "Department Stores Here and Abroad," *New York Times*, 21 September 1913, X16.

7 Crapsey, 1870, 96.

8 Nystrom, 1919, 209.

9 Proctor, 2006, 408.

10 Coles, 1999, 74.

11 Lancaster, 1995, 72.

12 "Chicago Real Estate. Marshall Field Plans New State Street Block," *Chicago Daily Times*, 7 October 1900, 35.

13 Siry, 1988, 191–92.

14 Marrey, 1979, fig. 225, 206–7.

15 Proctor, 2006, 398; Kathleen James, "From Messel to Mendelsohn: German department store architecture in defence of urban and economic change," in *Cathedrals of Consumption: the European Department Store, 1850–1939*, ed. Geoffrey Crossick and Serge Jaumain (Aldershot, England: Ashgate, 1999), 261–62.

16 Clausen, 1985, 25.

17 Andrew Ayers, *The Architecture of Paris* (Paris: Edition Axel Menges, 2004), 171.

18 Helga Kerp Behn, "Die Architektur des deutschen Warenhauses von ihren Anfängen bis 1933," Ph.D. dissertation, University of Cologne, 1984, 170–72.

19 Parnes, 1948, 231.

20 Margaret Leslie Davis, *Bullocks Wilshire* (Los Angeles: Balcony Press, 1996), 64.

21 Busbey, 1910, 158.

22 Santink, 1990, 101.

23 Helen Bullitt Lowry, "Art's New Job of Salesmanship," *New York Times*, 15 August 1920, 42.

24 Hooper, 1874, 466.

25 Marshall Cushing, *The Story of Our Post Office* (Boston: A. M. Thayer & Co., Publishers, 1893), 966–67.

26 James, 1999, 256; Henry, 1918, 144; Blanche McManus, *The American Woman Abroad* (New York: Dodd, Mead and Company, 1911), 200.

27 Philip Gilbert Hamerton, *Paris in Old and Present Times* (London: Seeley & Co. Ltd, 1907), 313–14.

28 Pound, 1960, 50.

29 Meredith L. Clausen, *Frantz Jourdain and the Samaritaine: Art Nouveau Theory and Criticism* (Leiden, The Netherlands: E. J. Brill, 1987), 1; Ayers, 2004, 29.

30 H. I. Brock, "Palace Settings for Modern Shoppers," *New York Times Sunday Magazine*, 3 May 1925, 12.

31 Hooper, 1874, 466; Very, 1875, 6.

32 Clausen, 1987, 4.

33 George B. Ford, "The Emancipation of Architecture in Belgium," *The American Architect*, 8 June 1907, 223.

34 James, 1999, 256.

35 Christoph Grunenberg, "Wonderland: Spectacles of Display from the Bon Marché to Prada," in *Shopping*, ed. Christoph Grunenberg and Max Hollein (Ostfildern, Germany: Hatje Cantz Publishers, 2002), 27.

36 "Art of Window Dressing," *New York Times Sunday Magazine*, 8 September 1901, 5; Siry, 1988, 5–6.

37 H. W. Desmond, "The Schlesinger & Mayer Building. Another View—What Mr. Louis Sullivan Stands For," *Architectural Record*, July 1904, 66.

38 Clausen, 1985, 24, 25.

39 Clausen, 1987, 281; Rosalind H. Williams, *Dream Worlds: Mass Consumption in Late Nineteenth-Century France* (Berkeley: University of California Press, 1982), 93–93.

40 "Immense Store in Berlin," *New York Times*, 5 November 1911, C4.

41 Behn, 1984, 110–17.

42 Max Creutz, *Das Warenhaus Tietz in Elberfeld* (Berlin: Ernst Wasmuth, 1912), 9; Wendt and Kogan, 1952, 263.

43 Gerlach, 1988, fig. 29; Creutz, 1912, 27, 37, 51–53.

44 "The 'Bon Marché' Drapery Establishment in Paris," *Warehousemen and Drapers' Trade Journal*, 24 October 1874, 520.

45 Cushing, 1893, 957.

46 Behn, 1984, figs. 68, 73, 77, 96, 111.

47 Spiekermann, 2000,162–63.

48 Patterson, 1906, 434.

49 G. B. Ford, "The 'Samaritaine' Department Store, Paris," *The American Architect and Building News*, 19 October 1907, 123.

50 Clausen, 1987, 215.

51 Hortense Odlum, *A Woman's Place: The Autobiography of Hortense Odlum* (New York: Charles Scribner's Sons, 1939), 64.

52 J. J., "Studio Talk," *The International Studio*, August 1909, 150.

53 Gerlach, 1988, 107; Behn, 1984, 117–18, figs. 128–31.

54 James, 1999, 256; David, 2003, 168.

55 Behn, 1984, figs. 22, 23, 24, 61, 62.

56 Ibid., 156–57.

57 Ibid., 157–58, fig. 206; 161, fig. 212; 158, fig. 207.

58 Iride Rosa and Andres Lepik, "Architecture: The Berlin-Tokyo Connection from late 19th Century to late 1920s," in exhibition catalog *Tokyo-Berlin/Berlin-Tokyo* (Tokyo: Mori Art Museum, 2006), 118–19, www.moriart.org/english/contents/tokyo-berlin/about/index.html.

59 Lungstrum, 1999, 136.

60 Behn, 1984, 226, fig. 307.

61 Ibid., 132, figs. 170–72.

62 Frei, 1997, 116.

63 James, 1999, 270; Al Chase, "Work to Start on Wieboldt's Million Dollar Department Store in River Forest," *Chicago Daily Times*, 21 July 1936, 20; Meredith Clausen, "The Department Store," in *Encyclopedia of Architecture: Design, Engineering and Construction*, vol. 2 (New York: John Wiley, 1988–90), 216–17.

64 Hunley Abbott, "The Store Building and Equipment," in *Twenty-Five Years of Retailing, 1911–1936*, 1936, 88–89.

65 Ayers, 2004, 171.

66 "Mr. Fred of the Lazari," *Fortune*, 37(3), March 1948, 108–15.

67 Parnes, 1948, 293.

68 Kenneth C. Welch, "Where Are Department Stores Going?" *Architectural Record*, November 1944, 94.

69 "New Store Design Called 'Hypnotic,'" *New York Times*, 7 July 1948, 33.

70 Parnes, 1948, 295.

71 "Fight Begun to Save Stuttgart Building," *New York Times*, 16 August 1959, 39.

72 Jonathan Glancey, "Top of the Blobs," *The Guardian*, www.guardian.co.uk, 1 September 2003.

73 "Foreign Office Architects' John Lewis in Leicester: Great Drapes," Martin Spring, *Building*, www.building.co.uk, Issue 17, 2008.

74 Anne-Marie O'Connor, "Nouvel wins the 2008 Pritzker Architecture Prize," latimes.com, 31 March 2008.

75 "Galeria Kaufhof," www.murphyjahn.com.

GETTING ATTENTION

1 Mahoney and Hession, 1949, 2.

2 Wischermann, 2000, 1; Cheney, 1983, 28.

3 Cushing, 1893, 969.

4 Ibid., 968.

5 "The Shops at Christmas Time," 1874, 644.

6 "Paris Shops at Easter," *Warehousemen and Drapers' Trade Journal*, 11 April 1874, 165.

7 Miller, 1981, 176.

8 Miller and Merrilees, 2004, 397; Santink, 1990, 179.

9 Robert Proctor, "A Cubist History: The Department Store in Late Nineteenth-Century Paris," *Transactions of the Royal Historical Society*, vol. 13, 2003, 228.

10 S. Hamada, "Selling Goods at Retail in Japan," *System*, XVII(1), 1910, 56.

11 Pound, 1960, 67.

12 Marvin Traub and Tom Teicholz, *Like No Other Store: The Bloomingdale's Legend and the Revolution in American Marketing* (New York: Random House/Times Books, 1993), 115.

13 Galeries Lafayette postcard, ca. 1906, author's collection.

14 Havens, 1994, 119.

15 Hamada, 1910, 56.

16 Ferry, 1960, 18.

17 Williams, 1982, 94.

18 C. Benedek, "The Paris of the Rising Franc," *The Living Age*, 1 March 1927, 389. Reprinted from *Neues Wiener Tagblatt*, Vienna, January 6.

19 "John Wanamaker," in *The Men Who Advertise* (New York: Nelson Chesman, Publishers, 1870), 33.

20 Cushing, 1893, 969.

21 Mahoney and Hession, 1949, 220.

22 Moeran, 1998, 150.

23 "Shopping in London," 1909, 24; Rappaport, 2000, 269, fn. 69.

24 Benedek, 1927, 389.

25 Clausen, 1987, 82–82.

26 Moeran, 1998, 150.

27 Richard S. Thornton, "Japanese Posters: The First 100 Years," *Design Issues*, VI(1), Fall 1989, 7, 8.

28 "Fairchild's, Paris, Says," *Men's Wear*, 29(2), 25 May 1910, 80.

29 Ernest Knaufft, "Art in Advertising," *Review of Reviews and the World's Work*, LXV(6), June 1922, 629.

30 Parnes, 1948, 221.

31 Alfred D. Chandler, Jr., *The Visible Hand* (Cambridge, MA: The Belknap Press, 1977), 228.

32 David, 2003, 166.

33 O'Brien, 1964, 30.

34 Rappaport, 2000, 156.

35 Cushing, 1893, 974.

36 "A Parisian Attraction," *Town & Country*, 10 December 1910, 79.

37 Moeran, 1998, 150–51.

38 Young, 1999, 57; Moeran, 1998, 148, 152–53.

39 Hamada, 1910, 56, 61.

40 Young, 1999, 57.

41 Appel, 1970, 406; Wendt and Kogan, 1952, 293.

42 Hepp, 2003, 99.

43 Nord, 1986, 69.

44 Child, 1884, 517–19.

45 Miller and Merrilees, 2004, 397.

46 "Romance in Great Shops," *New York Times*, 14 January 1883, 10.

47 "The Big Stores," *The Arena*, 22(2), Part 1, August 1899, 185; "Paris Merchant Loses $3,000,000 in a Panic," 1905, 2; Laurence Jerrold, "'Monsieur Parapluie,'" *The Monthly Review*, XXI(62), November, 1905, 134, 135.

48 Hepp, 2003, 100.

49 Cushing, 1893, 973.

50 "The Big Stores," *The Arena*, 22(2), Part 2, August 1899, 320.

51 Thomas Russell, *Commercial Advertising* (New York: G. P. Putnam's Sons, 1920), 173–74.

52 Dehn, 1899, 52. Author's translation.

53 Göhre, 1907, 39.

54 McManus, 1911, 199–200; "Department Stores Here and Abroad," 1913, X16.

55 Wanamaker advertisement, *Philadelphia Inquirer*, 19 June 1893, 8.

56 "Goodby, John!" *The Atlanta Constitution*, 22 June 1893, 4.

57 Moeran, 1998, 150.

58 Wright, 1918, 170.

59 "American Store Pleases London," *New York Times*, 18 April 1909, C4.

60 Robert W. Twyman, *Marshall Field & Co., 1852–1906* (Philadelphia: University of Pennsylvania Press, 1954), 149.

61 Louis Baury, "Art in Publicity," *The Bookman*, XXXVI(2), October 1912, 142; "American Store Pleases London," 1909, C4.

62 "London Department Stores Amalgamated," *Printers' Ink*, March 1920, 90.

63 Advertisements, *New York Times*, 14 March 1929, 15, and 15 March 1929, 15; "Business & Finance: Holy Ghost," *Time*, 25 March 1929, no page numbers, accessed via www.Time.com.

64 Hilton, 2004, 950.

65 Christina Kiaer, "Rodchenko in Paris," *October*, vol. 75, Winter 1996, 24.

66 Hilton, 2004, 951.

67 Taft, 1929, 2.

68 Knaufft, 1922, 625.

69 Alfred Yockney, "Some Recent London Posters," *International Studio*, LIV(216), February 1915, 281–82.

70 Béatrice de Andia and Caroline François, *Les Cathédrales du Commerce parisien: Grands Magasins et enseignes* (Paris: Action Artistique de la Ville de Paris, 2006), 138.
71 *Harper's Bazaar* advertisement, *Printers' Ink*, 28 September 1922, 37.
72 Cushing, 1893, 970.
73 Louvre advertisement, *Town & Country*, 10 June 1911, 89.
74 Harris, 1994, 182.
75 "Dallas in Wonderland: Neiman Marcus Company," *Fortune*, 16(5), November 1937, 116–17.
76 Mahoney and Hession, 1949, 220.
77 Linda L. Tyler, "'Commerce and Poetry Hand in Hand': Music in American Department Stores, 1880–1930," *Journal of the American Musicological Society*, 45, 1992, 92.
78 Pound, 1960, 184.
79 Mahoney and Hession, 1949, 117.
80 Havens, 1994, 69.
81 Mahoney and Hession, 1949, 210.
82 Charles Edward Russell, *These Shifting Scenes* (New York: Hodder & Stoughton/ G. H. Doran Company, 1914), 309–10.
83 Jason Rogers, *Building Newspaper Advertising* (New York: Harper & Bros., 1919), 187–88.
84 Taft, 1929, 40.
85 Wood, 1987, 198–99.
86 Pound, 1960, 101.
87 Mahoney and Hession, 1949, 154.
88 Santink, 1990, 181.
89 Knaufft, 1922, 627.
90 Eaton's advertisement for its 75th anniversary, *The Lethbridge Herald*, 7 December 1944, back page.
91 Jerrold, 1905, 181.
92 Earnest Elmo Calkins, *The Business of Advertising* (New York: D. Appleton and Company, 1915), 164.
93 Rappaport, 2000, 158.
94 George Hough Perry, "The Fundamentals of Introductory Advertising," in *Seventh Annual Convention of the Associated Advertising Clubs of America* (Boston: Pilgrim Publicity Association, 1912), 386.
95 Mahoney and Hession, 1949, 195.
96 Marcus, 1974, 228–29.
97 Ibid.
98 Millie R. Creighton, "Maintaining Cultural Boundaries in Retailing: How Japanese Department Stores Domesticate 'Things Foreign,'" *Modern Asian Studies*, 25(4), 1991, 692.

WINDOW GAZING

1 Roman Paddison, Anne Findlay, and Allen Findlay, "Shop Windows as an Indicator of Retail Modernity in the Third World," *Area*, 16(3), 1984.
2 Uwe Spiekermann, "Display Windows and Window Displays in German Cities of the Nineteenth Century: Towards the History of a Commercial Breakthrough," in *Advertising and the European City: Historical Perspectives*, ed. Clemens Wischermann and Elliott Shore (Aldershot, England: Ashgate, 2000), 165.
3 Ibid.
4 Letter to the editor from "An Old Cockney," "Shop Windows on Holidays," *The Times*, 27 March 1894, 6.
5 "The Shop Windows of Paris," *The Times*, 11 March 1957, 13.
6 Frei, 1997, 141.
7 Siry, 1988, 37.
8 Parnes, 1948, 159.
9 Spiekermann, 2000, 155–56.
10 Lancaster, 1995, 55–56.
11 Hamada, 1910, 61.
12 Pound, 1960, 71.
13 Sherwin Simmons, "August Macke's Shoppers: Commodity Aesthetics, Modernist Autonomy and the Inexhaustible Will of Kitsch," *Zeitschrift für Kunstgeschichte*, 63(1), 2000, 50–51.
14 Sara K. Schneider, *Vital Mummies: Performance Design for the Show-Window Mannequin* (New Haven: Yale University Press, 1995), 11.
15 Lucy H. Hooper, "Shopping in Paris," *Lippincott's Magazine*, June 1871, 574; Hooper, 1874, 466.

16 Crapsey, 1870, 95.
17 "The Spectator," *The Outlook*, 58(5), 29 January 1898, 266.
18 Rappaport, 2000, 151; Leach, 1989, 106; "Daniells," *The New Yorker*, 1 September 1928, 10–11; Hooper, 1874, 465.
19 Frederick Kiesler, *Contemporary Art Applied to the Store and Its Display* (New York: Brentano's, 1930).
20 Patterson, 1906, 432, 434–35.
21 Twyman, 1954, 152; Lancaster, 1995, 65.
22 Leach, 1993, 55–61.
23 Nathaniel C. Fowler, Jr., *About Advertising and Printing* (Boston: L. Barta & Co., Publishers, 1889), 116; "The Spectator," 1898, 265.
24 "Queer Work for Women," *Washington Post*, 8 May 1898, 24.
25 "Shopping in London," 1909, 24.
26 "Crowds and Shop Windows," *The Times*, 2 November 1910, 8.
27 Leach, 1993, 70; Mahoney and Hession, 1949, 218.
28 A. P. Johnson, ed. and comp., *Library of Advertising* (Chicago: Cree Publishing Company, 1911), 32–34.
29 Leonard Marcus, *The American Store Window* (New York: Watson-Guptill, 1978), 20.
30 "Window Displays Here and Abroad," *New York Times*, 31 August 1913, S5.
31 Johnson, 1911, 50.
32 Lungstrum, 1999, 132–33.
33 Marcus, 1978, 25, 28; Schneider, 1995, 11–12.
34 "New Art Displays Steadily Growing," *New York Times*, 5 February 1928, 49.
35 Lancaster, 1995, 67–68; Karal Ann Marling, *Merry Christmas! Celebrating America's Greatest Holiday* (Cambridge, MA: Harvard University Press, 2000), 96; Jonneke Jobse, *De Stijl Continued* (Rotterdam: 010 Publishers, 2005), 34.
36 Odlum, 1939, 165–67.
37 Hellmut [sic] Wohl, "Marcel Duchamp in Newark," *The Burlington Magazine*, 145(1198), January 2003, 36.
38 Ministère du Commerce, *Rapports du Jury International* (Paris: Imprimerie Nationale, 1902), 330.
39 Schneider, 1995, 12.
40 Marcus, 1978, 30.
41 Charles J. Shevlin, "Trends in Display," *Journal of Retailing*, October 1944, 65–66.
42 "Store Windows Reflecting Yule Spirit Draw Many Letters of Appreciation," *New York Times*, 14 December 1944, 26.
43 Schneider, 1995, 47, 116.
44 Peggy Durkin, "Department Store: Clue to the New Japan," *New York Times Sunday Magazine*, 5 October 1958, 13.
45 Sally Heinemann, "What's Going on in the Windows?" *New York Times*, 28 November 1976, 165.
46 Suzanne Slesin, "He Really Does Windows," *New York Times*, 8 December 1988, C1.
47 Bruce Weber, "Barneys Halts Store Display of Pop Crèche in Window," *New York Times*, 13 December 1994, B3.

MERCHANDISING SPECTACLES

1 Nord, 1986, 73–74.
2 Parnes, 1948, 160.
3 "America To-Day. Yankee Department Stores," 1905, 9.
4 Child, 1884, 515.
5 Illustration in de Andia, 2006, 103.
6 Ibid., 104.
7 See, for example, postcards and drawings in de Andia, 2006.
8 Charles Jenner store in Edinburgh, as depicted in Alexandra Artley, ed., *The Golden Age of Shop Design: European Shop Interiors 1880–1939* (New York: Whitney Library of Design, 1976), 20–21, 23.
9 Nystrom, 1919, 213.
10 Artley, 1976, 20–21.
11 Gibbons, 1926, 80–81.
12 Lancaster, 1995, 80.
13 Ken W. Parker, "Sign Consumption in the 19th-Century Department Store. An Examination of Visual Merchandising

in the Grand Emporiums (1846–1900)," *Journal of Sociology*, 39(4), 2003, 360.
14 1920 Bon Marché photograph in de Andia, 2006, 49.
15 Tietz photographs, Frei, 1997, 141; Tietz, 1965, 68.
16 Artley, 1976, 54–55, 110.
17 Crossick and Jaumain, 1999, 27.
18 Parker, 2003, 363, 364.
19 Creighton, 1991, 681–82.
20 Robert A. M. Stern et al., *New York 1930: Architecture and Urbanism Between the Two World Wars* (New York: Rizzoli, 1987), 336.
21 Leach, 1993, 83.
22 Wendt and Kogan, 1952, 306–7.
23 Tony Morgan, *Visual Merchandising: Window and In-Store Displays for Retail* (London: Laurence King Publishing, 2008), 156.
24 Martin M. Pegler, *Visual Merchandising and Display*, 5th ed. (New York: Fairchild Publications, 2006), 43.

SERVICES AND CIRCUSES

1 Robert Spector, *More Than a Store: Frederick & Nelson, 1890 to 1990* (Bellevue, Washington: Documentary Book Publishers Corp., 1990); Pasdermadjian, 1954, 124–26; Pound, 1960, 107.
2 Nystrom, 1919, 220.
3 Ibid.
4 Resseguie, 1965, 321.
5 "What Does It Cost to Keep a Customer? *New York Times Sunday Magazine*, 31 March 1912, 13.
6 Young, 1999, 62.
7 Ibid., 55–56.
8 Gustav Streseman, quoted in Grunenberg, 2002, 22.
9 Pound, 1960, 107.
10 "A New Enterprise," 1906, 56.
11 Very, 1875, 6; "The Shops at Christmas Time," 1874, 644.
12 Very, 1875, 6; "Best Managed City of Europe," 1903, 46; George Grosz, *George Grosz: An Autobiography*, trans. Nora Hodges (Berkeley: University of California Press, 1998), 89–90.
13 Twyman, 1954, 124.
14 "American Store Pleases London," 1909, C4.
15 Alfred Marshall Hitchcock, *Over Japan Way* (New York: Henry Holt & Company, 1917), 253.
16 Lyndon P. Smith, "An Attempt to Give a Functional Expression to the Architecture of a Department Store," Part I of "The Schlesinger & Mayer Building," *Architectural Record*, July 1904, 53–60.
17 Alfred Lief, *Family Business: A Century in the Life and Times of Strawbridge & Clothier* (New York: McGraw-Hill, 1968), 186.
18 Göhre, 1907, 95; Mahoney and Hession, 1949, 87.
19 *A Friendly Guide Book to Philadelphia and the Wanamaker Store* (Philadelphia: John Wanamaker, 1926), 53; "Gimbel Revisions Called Store Aid," *New York Times*, 19 August 1951, 119.
20 Tietz, 1965, 107.
21 "Spring Fashions," *Warehousemen and Drapers' Trade Journal*, 28 March 1874, 140.
22 "The Shops at Christmas Time," 1874, 644.
23 Erika D. Rappaport, "'The Halls of Temptation': Gender, Politics, and the Construction of the Department Store in Late Victorian London," *Journal of British Studies*, 35(1), January 1996, 74.
24 "Women Threaten a Boycott," *New York Times*, 16 November 1894, 8.
25 Wendt and Kogan, 1952, 338; Jean Maddern Pitrone, *Hudson's: Hub of America's Heartland* (West Bloomfield, MI: Altwerger Co. 1991), 135.
26 Child, 1884, 516.
27 "Best Managed City of Europe," 1903, 46.
28 Pound, 1960, 70.
29 Moeran, 1998, 159.
30 "The Marshall Field's of Tokyo," *The Native American*, No. 28, March 1914, 168.

31 Wright, 1918, 166.
32 Moeran, 1998, 159–60.
33 Sam Jameson, "Toyko Store Takes Care of Customers, Even After Death," *Los Angeles Times*, 10 March 1977, B14.
34 Ferry, 1960, 338; "Splendour at Banquet," *The Canberra Times*, 5 February 1954, 2.
35 "A Parisian Attraction," *Town & Country*, 10 December 1910, 79.
36 Louis E. Schleber, *The Modern Store* (Boston: The Lamson Co. 1916), 33; Roberta Morgan, *It's Better at Burdine's* (Miami: The Pickering Press, 1991), 35.
37 Photo postcard of the Bon Marché, author's collection.
38 Moeran, 1998, 160.
39 Young, 1999, 62; Folder labeled "Filene's Oddities," in Filene's Marketing Archives, Boston Public Library, Cabinet 12, Drawer 3.
40 News photograph, author's collection.
41 Mahoney and Hession, 1949, 100; "John Wanamaker," 1889, 117.
42 Moeran, 1998, 159; Patterson, 1906, 438; Leach, 1993, 138.
43 W. L. Pollard, "Service Features Dominate American Retailing," *Pacific Ports*, September 1922, 53.
44 *Customer Services Provided by Department and Specialty Stores* (New York: National Retail Merchants Association, 1964), 23.
45 J. Pollen, "Russia and Esperanto," *Proceedings Anglo-Russian Literary Society*, 6 April 1909, 42.
46 "John Wanamaker," 1889, 117.
47 Georges d'Avenel, *Le Mécanisme de la vie moderne* (Paris: Librairie Armand Colin, 1906), 61.
48 Miller, 1981, 61–62.
49 Santink, 1990, 226; Geoffrey Crossick and Serge Jaumain, "The World of the Department Store: Distribution, Culture and Social Change," in *Cathedrals of Consumption: The European Department Store, 1850–1939*, ed. Geoffrey Crossick and Serge Jaumain (Aldershot, England: Ashgate, 1999), 13; Moeran, 1998, 150.
50 Ferry, 1960, 20.
51 Patterson, 1906, 428.
52 Crossick and Jaumain, 1999, 13; Robert J. Epstein, "The Story of Fox's, 1847–1947," MA thesis, Columbia University School of Business, 1948, 116.
53 1892 letter, in *Letters of Anton Chekhov to His Family and Friends*, trans. Constance Garnett (New York: The Macmillan Company, 1920), 318.
54 Richard Burbidge, "Running a Store in War Time," in *Managing a Business in War Time* (Chicago: A. W. Shaw Company, 1918), 96.
55 "The 'Bon Marché' Drapery Establishment in Paris," 1874, 520.
56 Moeran, 1998, 150.
57 Sams, 1917, 40.
58 Burbidge, 1918, 94.
59 "Evaluation of Services to Customers," *Journal of Retailing*, October 1929, 25–26.
60 Havens, 1994, 60.
61 "Stewart, Alexander Turney," 1897, 352.
62 "The Universal Provider," 1887, 2.
63 Dickens, 1878, 83.
64 "Macy's Leisurama," *New York Times Magazine*, 4 August 2002, 50.
65 Frank Riley, "Harrods Is Magic in the Kingdom," *Los Angeles Times*, 12 August 1979, E3.
66 Harrods advertisement, *The Bystander*, 19 December 1906, iv.
67 Wendt and Kogan, 1952, 360–61; Jane Geniesse, "What Have You Got in Louis Quinze? And Charge It, Please," *New York*, 25 September 1972, 43.
68 Wendt and Kogan, 1952, 362.
69 Harrods advertisement, *The Scottish Geographical Magazine*, XXI(4), April 1906, 172.
70 Child, 1884, 516.
71 Grosz, 1998, 89–90.
72 Wright, 1918, 168; Lancaster, 1995, 96.
73 Lancaster, 1995, 96; Hordern's advertisement, *Sydney Morning Herald*, 10 January 1936.

74 Webb Miller, "London, Europe's Most Vulnerable Capital, Prepares for War," *Abilene Reporter News*, 15 June 1938, 12.
75 "Stores Go into Show Business," *Business Week*, October 1954, 46.
76 Very, 1875, 6.
77 Herbert Ershkowitz, *John Wanamaker, Philadelphia Merchant* (Conshohocken, PA: Combined Publishing, 1999), 114.
78 Göhre, 1907, 116.
79 Moeran, 1998, 162.
80 Reilly, 1966, 172.
81 Parnes, 1948, 89.
82 Merin, 1983, G22.
83 Miller, 1981, 171.
84 Ershkowitz, 1999, 118.
85 Tyler, 1992, 75.
86 Ibid.
87 Wright, 1918, 170.
88 Stewart Cullin, "Department Store Called Our Greatest Influence," *Women's Wear*, no. 3, 22 November 1926, 6ff.; "Department Stores," *Washington Post*, 20 September 1928, 6.
89 W. L. Pollard, "How American Department Stores Cultivate Trade," *Pacific Ports*, August 1922, 116.
90 Creighton, 1991, 691.
91 Hilton, 2004, 953.
92 Lancaster, 1995, 80.
93 Pound, 1960, 209–10.
94 Captain Arthur Sweetser and Lieutenant Gordon Lamont, *Opportunities in Aviation* (New York: Harper & Brothers, 1920), 77.
95 Advertisement in *The Jewish Criterion*, 25 May 1928, 56.
96 Very, 1875, 6.
97 "New Art Gallery," *Boston Daily Globe*, 29 March 1894, 3.
98 Georges-Louis Peuch, "Kunst zu Gast im Kaufhof," *Die Zeit*, 13 September 1968 (accessed via Zeit Online, www.zeit.de, 2).
99 Lancaster, 1995, 80.
100 Hi Simons, "At Chicago," *The Arts*, November 1921, 95.
101 Aaron Sheon, "1913: Forgotten Cubist Exhibitions in America," *Arts Magazine*, March 1983, 93; Leach, 1993, 136.
102 Leach, 1993, 137.
103 "What's in Store—Greek, Roman Art," *Washington Post*, 19 September 1965, F19.
104 Peuch, 1968 (Zeit Online, 2).
105 Alfred Marshall Hitchcock, *Over Japan Way* (New York: Henry Holt & Company, 1917, 252–53; Sams, 1917, 40.
106 "Department Store: Clue to the New Japan," 1958, 13.
107 A. M. Rosenthal, "Tokyo Department Stores Spur Sales with Cultural Exhibitions. Displays of Flower Arrangements, Folk Craft, Paintings and Sculpture Seem to Make Cash Registers Ring," *New York Times*, 23 October 1961, 3.
108 Havens, 1994, 79.
109 "Eaton's Santa Claus Parade," Archives of Ontario, www.archives.gov.on.ca.
110 Leigh Eric Schmidt, *Consumer Rites: The Buying and Selling of American Holidays* (Princeton, NJ: Princeton University Press, 1995), 145.
111 "Greet Santa Claus as 'King of Kiddies,'" *New York Times*, 28 November 1924, 15.

POSTSCRIPT

1 Nystrom, 1932, 155–56.

Selected Bibliography

de Andia, Béatrice, Caroline François, et al. *Les Cathédrales du Commerce parisien: Grands Magasins et enseignes.* Paris: Action Artistique de la Ville de Paris, 2006.

Appel, Joseph H. *The Business Biography of John Wanamaker.* 1930. Reprint. New York: AMS Press, 1970.

d'Avenel, Georges. *Le Mécanisme de la vie moderne.* Paris: Librairie Armand Colin, 1906.

Behn, Helga Kerp. "Die Architektur des deutschen Warenhauses von ihren Anfängen bis 1933." Doctoral dissertation, University of Cologne, 1984.

Bird, William L., Jr. *Holidays on Display.* New York: Princeton Architectural Press, 2007.

Cheney, David. "The Department Store as a Cultural Form." *Theory, Culture & Society,* 1(3), 1983, 22–31.

Clausen, Meredith L. "The Department Store—Development of the Type." *Journal of Architectural Education,* 39(1), Autumn 1985, 20–29.

———. *Frantz Jourdain and the Samaritaine: Art Nouveau Theory and Criticism.* Leiden: E. J. Brill, 1987.

Creutz, Max. *Das Warenhaus Tietz in Elberfeld.* Berlin: Ernst Wasmuth, 1912.

Crossick, Geoffrey, and Serge Jaumain, eds. *Cathedrals of Consumption: The European Department Store, 1850–1939.* Aldershot, England: Ashgate, 1999.

David, Anthony. *The Patron: A Life of Salman Schocken, 1877–1959.* New York: Metropolitan Books/Henry Holt, 2003.

Davis, Margaret Leslie. *Bullocks Wilshire.* Los Angeles: Balcony Press, 1996.

Dehn, Paul. *Die Grossbazare und Massenzweiggeschäfte.* Berlin: Trowitzsch, 1899.

Ershkowitz, Herbert. *John Wanamaker: Philadelphia Merchant.* Conshohocken, PA: Combined Publishing, 1999.

Ferry, John William. *A History of the Department Store.* New York: Macmillan, 1960.

Frei, Helmut. *Tempel der Kauflust: Eine Geschichte der Warenhauskultur.* Leipzig: Edition Leipzig, 1997.

Gerlach, Siegfried. *Das Warenhaus in Deutschland. Seine Entwicklung bis zum ersten Weltkrieg in historisch-geographischer Sicht.* Stuttgart: Franz Steiner Verlag, 1988.

Göhre, Paul. *Das Warenhaus.* Frankfurt am Main: Literarische Anstalt/Rütten & Loening, 1907.

Grunenberg, Christoph, and Max Hollein, eds. *Shopping: A Century of Art and Consumer Culture.* Ostfildern, Germany: Hatje Cantz Verlag, 2002.

Harris, Leon. *Merchant Princes: An Intimate History of Jewish Families Who Built Great Department Stores.* New York: HarperCollins, 1979; New York: Kodansha International, 1994.

Havens, Thomas R. H. *Architecture of Affluence: The Tsutsumi Family and the Seibu-Saison Enterprise in Twentieth-Century Japan.* Cambridge, MA: Harvard UniversityPress, 1994.

Hendrickson, Robert. *The Grand Emporiums: The Illustrated History of America's Great Department Stores.* New York: Stein and Day, 1979.

Hilton, Marjorie L. "Retailing the Revolution: The State Department Store (GUM) and Soviet Society in the 1920s." *Journal of Social History,* 37(4), 2004, 939–64.

Hower, Ralph M. *History of Macy's of New York 1858–1919.* Cambridge, MA: Harvard University Press, 1943.

Lancaster, William. *The Department Store: A Social History.* London: Leicester University Press, 1995.

Leach, William. *Land of Desire: Merchants, Power, and the Rise of a New American Culture.* New York: Vintage Books, 1994.

Lenz, Rudolf. *Karstadt: Ein deutscher Warenhauskonzern, 1920–1950.* Stuttgart: Deutsche Verlags-Anstalt, 1995.

Lungstrum, Janet Ward. "The Display Window: Designs and Desires of Weimar Consumerism." *New German Critique,* no. 76, Winter 1999, 115–60.

MacPherson, Kerrie L., ed. *Asian Department Stores.* Honolulu: University of Hawaii Press, 1998.

Mahoney, Tom, and Rita Hession. *Public Relations for Retailers.* New York: The Macmillan Co., 1949.

Marcus, Leonard. *The American Store Window.* New York: Watson-Guptill, 1978.

Marcus, Stanley. *Minding the Store.* Boston: Little, Brown & Co., 1974.

Marrey, Bernard. *Les grands magasins des origines à 1939.* Paris: Librairies Picard, 1979.

Miller, Michael Barry. *The Bon Marché: Bourgeois Culture and the Department Store, 1869–1920.* Princeton, NJ: Princeton University Press, 1981.

Nord, Philip G. *Paris Shopkeepers and the Politics of Resentment.* Princeton, NJ: Princeton University Press, 1986.

Nystrom, Paul. *The Economics of Retailing.* New York: The Ronald Press, 1919.

———. *The Economics of Retailing: Retail Institutions and Trends.* 3rd ed. New York: The Ronald Press, 1932.

Parnes, Louis. *Planning Stores That Pay: Organic Design and Layout for Efficient Merchandising.* New York: F. W. Dodge Corporation, 1948.

Pasdermadjian, Hrant. *The Department Store: Its Origins, Evolution and Economics.* London: Newman Books, 1954.

Phillips, Wesley B. *How Department Stores Are Carried On.* New York: Dodd, Mead, 1901.

Pound, Reginald. *Selfridge: A Biography.* London: Heinemann, 1960.

Proctor, Robert. "Constructing the Retail Monument: The Parisian Department Store and Its Property, 1855–1914." *Urban History,* 33(3), 2006, 393–410.

Rappaport, Erika Diane. *Shopping for Pleasure: Women in the Making of London's West End.* Princeton, NJ: Princeton University Press, 2000.

Resseguie, Harry E. "Alexander Turney Stewart and the Development of the Department Store, 1823–1876." *The Business History Review,* 39(3), Autumn 1965, 301–22.

Santink, Joy L. *Timothy Eaton and the Rise of His Department Store.* Toronto: University of Toronto Press, 1990.

Siry, Joseph. *Carson Pirie Scott: Louis Sullivan and the Chicago Department Store.* Chicago: University of Chicago Press, 1988.

Tietz, Georg. *Hermann Tietz: Geschichte einer Familie und ihrer Warenhäuser.* Stuttgart: Deutsche Verlags-Anstalt, 1965.

Traub, Marvin, and Tom Teicholz. *Like No Other Store… : The Bloomingdale's Legend and the Revolution in American Marketing.* New York: Random House/Times Books, 1993.

Twyman, Robert, W. *Marshall Field & Co., 1852–1906.* Philadelphia: University of Pennsylvania Press, 1954.

Wendt, Lloyd, and Herman Kogan. *Give the Lady What She Wants!: The Story of Marshall Field & Company.* Chicago: Rand McNally Co., 1952.

Whitaker, Jan. *Service and Style: How the American Department Store Fashioned the Middle Class.* New York: St. Martin's Press, 2006.

Williams, Rosalind H. *Dream Worlds: Mass Consumption in Late Nineteenth-Century France.* Berkeley: University of California Press, 1982.

Wischermann, Clemens, and Elliott Shore, eds. *Advertising and the European City: Historical Perspectives.* Aldershot, England: Ashgate, 2000.

Wood, James M. *Halle's: Memoirs of a Family Department Store (1891–1982).* Cleveland: Geranium Press, 1987.

Young, Louise. "Marketing the Modern Department Stores, Consumer Culture, and the New Middle Class in Interwar Japan." *International Labor and Working-Class History,* no. 55, Spring 1999, 52–70.

Index